THE ANGEL
AND THE CHOLENT

Raphael Patai Series in Jewish Folklore and Anthropology

General Editor

Dan Ben-Amos
University of Pennsylvania

the ANGEL *and the* CHOLENT

Food Representation from the Israel Folktale Archives

Idit Pintel-Ginsberg

WAYNE STATE UNIVERSITY PRESS

DETROIT

ISBN 978-0-8143-4884-0 (paperback)
ISBN 978-0-8143-4885-7 (case)
ISBN 978-0-8143-4886-4 (ebook)

Library of Congress Cataloging Number: 2021938755

Published with support from the fund for the Raphael Patai Series in Jewish
Folklore and Anthropology.

On cover: "When the Messiah Comes, the Righteous Will Feast on the
Leviathan" by Mayer Kirshenblatt (1916–2009). From Mayer Kirshenblatt and
Barbara Kirshenblatt-Gimblett, *They Called Me Mayer July: Painted Memories of
Jewish Childhood in Poland Before the Holocaust* (University of California Press,
2007). Courtesy of Barbara Kirshenblatt-Gimblett. Cover design by Mindy
Basinger Hill.

Wayne State University Press rests on Waawiyaataanong, also referred to
as Detroit, the ancestral and contemporary homeland of the Three Fires
Confederacy. These sovereign lands were granted by the Ojibwe, Odawa,
Potawatomi, and Wyandot Nations, in 1807, through the Treaty of Detroit.
Wayne State University Press affirms Indigenous sovereignty and honors all
tribes with a connection to Detroit. With our Native neighbors, the press
works to advance educational equity and promote a better future for the earth
and all people.

Wayne State University Press
Leonard N. Simons Building
4809 Woodward Avenue
Detroit, Michigan 48201-1309

Visit us online at wsupress.wayne.edu

In memory of my mother,
Tauba Pintel, née Goldman,
whose dishes I will long
for all my life.

A King asked his guests during a banquet, "What is the best music?"

The guests gave various answers, but none of them satisfied the King.

The King signaled to the head chef to begin serving the fragrant dishes to the table. And indeed, as soon as they brought them, the serving vessels clanged and immediately the guests started to rejoice.

"You see," said the King, "this is the best music!"

The Best Music, IFA 3563 (told by Esther Bina Rochfeld, Poland; recorded by Zvi Moshe Haimovits)

Contents

4. IT IS KOSHER AND FIT TO EAT: FOOD AND KASHRUT   109

5. FISH IN HONOR OF THE SHABBAT: FOOD AND SACRED TIME   141

PREFACE

F ood has a cardinal presence in human life: essential to physical existence and inseparable from daily routine. Food is also a central component of society—it reflects social structure and its various strata (Counihan 1999; Douglas 1984; Mintz and Du Bois 2002) and is woven into symbols and rituals (Lévi-Strauss 1997). Food expresses a broad spectrum of identities: national, ethnic, economic, and gender (Long 2015; M. Jones 2007; Mintz and Du Bois 2002; Muhawi and Kanaana 1989; Myerhoff 1978; Goode 1992; Fischler 1988). It acts as an accessible language to all while at the same time constituting an intricate system of communication (Barthes 1957, 1961; Sutton 2001, 2010).

This book examines the ways folktales reflect customs, beliefs, and cultural perceptions related to food. According to Michael Owen Jones, researchers in fields related to nutrition have paid "too little attention to the traditional and symbolic aspects of food in people's day-to-day activities" (2007, 162). As Kara Keeling and Scott Pollard suggest, examining folktales as a literary trope or as a cultural signifier while focusing on food enriches the interpretation of the texts (2020).

Folktales are a creation and expression of a society and its individuals (see Ben-Amos 1992). Occasionally they enunciate identification with and acceptance of a society's beliefs and norms, but at times they confront them, question them, and even reject them (Yassif 2009). A folktale is also a vehicle of the storyteller's voice. Even when the tale refers to a well-known phenomenon in the society, it expresses the storyteller's own experience or the concept that he or she intends to convey by means of the narrative

(Alexander 2008). The narration's main process is the verbal conveyance of the storyteller's memories and imagination, via extremely limited performing resources and time frame.

Food is an inseparable part of reality and its various aspects are as well known to all, almost intuitively, as its smell and taste. Therefore folktales related to food often provide only hints and implicit references to food, with the expectation that their full connotations will naturally occur in the audience's imagination. However, as folktales emanate from creative imagination, they are not restricted to realistic representations of food. Therefore they do not necessarily bear an immediate and direct reflection of foodways.

Fantastic and supernatural elements are present in some tales; these, of course, can't be taken as part of the society's real life (Archer, Turley, and Thomas 2014). A tale may recall an ancient but vanished technology related to food preparation. In some instances, a tale about food may be offered as a substitute for real food, to satisfy real hunger. An extreme example of this is the testimony about the exchange of elaborate recipes among starving women incarcerated in concentration camps during World War II (De Silva 2006; German 2011; Gilbert 2014; Shahani 2018, 6–7).

The thirty folktales included in this book originate from the folktales collection compiled by the Israel Folktale Archives (IFA), named in honor of Dov Noy, at the University of Haifa. They were chosen from a group of 180 tales whose plots relate to food. The key for the choice was based on various parameters: foremost, their pertinence to the subject and the fact that they were not previously published; secondarily, to present an extended variety of ethnic groups and topics relating to food. These thirty folktales were registered over a forty-year period, mostly from 1957 to 1995, except for two that were recorded in 2004.

Dov Noy founded IFA in 1955 as part of the Haifa Municipality's Museum of Ethnology and Folklore. Noy's main goals were, first, to collect a large pool of folktales from Jews and gentiles in Israel in order to establish a basis for academic research and study of folk literature and, second, to preserve the folk literature of Jewish immigrants inundating the young State of Israel between the years 1948 and 1957, when over nine hundred thousand arrived. His concern was that this rich oral heritage might vanish with the immigrants' transition to a new language and modern lifestyle (Hasan-Rokem 1999). Noy created a network of folktale collectors, comprising family members, school pupils, and his own academic students (Bar-Itzhak 2013, 2019; Hasan-Rokem 1998; Hasan-Rokem and Yassif 1989; Schrire 2011). At this early stage, IFA focused primarily on the tales themselves as heritage. These folktales where recorded at the initiative of the collectors and narrated under academic circumstances (compared to a more natural and spontaneous setting such as a family gathering or get-together with friends).

Two extensive fieldwork projects, held during the years 1979–81 in the development towns of Beit Shean and Shlomi yielded a compilation of four hundred folktales (Bar-Itzhak and Shenhar 1993a, 1993b).

Nowadays IFA continues to record folktales from among newly arrived immigrant groups—from the former Soviet Union (Fialkova and Elenevskaya 2007) and Ethiopia (Milo 2019)—as well as from Israel's Arab society (Meron 2005–12; Dehamshe 2017). Currently, IFA has cataloged over twenty-five thousand folktales; two thousand of them are from non-Jewish groups living in Israel (Druze, Bedouin, Circassians, Muslims, and Christian Arabs). Tales from IFA's collection were sorted by the archives' researchers into seventy different ethnic groups, according to the storytellers' lands of origin. This collection is the largest assemblage of Jewish folk literature in the world. In 2017, IFA's collection was included in UNESCO's "Memory of the World" program.

Numerous folktales from the IFA collection have been translated and published in various languages: English (Alexander 2008; Noy 1963a, 1965a; 1966b; Shenhar 1987), German (Jason and Gassmann 1976; Noy 1963b); Arabic (Meron 2005–12), French (Noy 1965b, 1968), Spanish (Noy 1965c, 1966a). The three-volume work by Dan Ben-Amos, *Folktales of the Jews*, is one of the most extensively edited collections of IFA folktales, translated into English and thoroughly annotated. The most recent publication, IFA's jubilee book, *The Power of a Tale*, (Bar-Itzhak and Pintel-Ginsberg 2019), contains over fifty tales translated into English, each one interpreted and analyzed by researchers from Israel and the United States. It offers a vast spectrum of research in the field.

The folktales presented here were told by twenty-nine storytellers from seventeen different locales or ethnic groups (Argentina [1 tale], Belarus [1], Bulgaria [1], Egypt [1], Israeli Muslim [1], Israeli Sephardic [1], Italy [1], Kurdistan Iraq [1], Libya [1], Lithuania [2], Morocco [3], Persia [1], Poland [7], Russia [3], Turkey [2], Ukraine [1], and Yemen [2]), representing the cultural and thematic wealth of the archives' collection. All of them, except one, were told by Jewish storytellers; the exception was recorded from an Israeli Muslim storyteller. The tales' common denominator is their connection to food.

This book is composed of five chapters, each one preceded by a short introduction. In each chapter the tales, translated into English from their original language, are presented as they were told; the translation tries to reflect the oral character of the tales. Each tale is followed by a discussion containing brief biographical information about the storyteller as recorded at the IFA archives, although in some cases no information is provided. The discussion also includes an extended commentary on the text. Although there is value in the tales alone, the introductions and commentaries offer a wider and deeper understanding of the cultural, historical, and religious contexts in which they were told. Presented and explained, the tales provide an entry into Jewish culture and its traditions.

The first chapter deals with the sensuous pleasure of eating and explores its boundaries. As food was often scarce and hard to come by for Jews, there is a respectful attitude toward tasty and fine foods. In a usually humoristic manner, gluttony is questioned, mostly criticized, although in one instance it is surprisingly approved. On the other hand, the spoiling of food, even with a religiously oriented intention, is mocked and subtly rejected.

The second chapter discusses gender issues depicted in folktales relating to food. It focuses on gender's intricate meanings: gender identity and definition of it by food, the various roles assigned to food preparation and consumption by each gender, the power struggles between the sexes, and food's sexual symbolism.

The third chapter focuses on the social aspects of food: its role in social systems and encounters between them, its indication of economic and social status, its reinforcement of social bonding, and even its capacity to save lives through shared meals. The chapter also deals with the resentment and violence that hunger may erupt in.

The fourth chapter deals with the connection between food and group identity, specifically as an element in Jewish culture and by way of its dietary rules. The various reasons for these rules are described in the chapter's introduction. Some are pragmatic in nature, such as hygiene and food safety, and some social in nature, employed to strengthen one's identity and affinity with the group. Lastly, the fifth chapter looks at the correlation between food and sacred time, its role and characteristics as related to ritual observance. Central here is the preparation of special dishes and their meaning for Shabbat, the most frequently observed sacred time in the Jewish year.

Each chapter includes folktales related to its specific topic. However, as typical of the folk oeuvre, which by nature is complex, intricate, and resistant to conforming to scientific theories and categories, some of the tales might well have been included simultaneously in several chapters.

ACKNOWLEDGMENTS

Special thanks go to my friend and colleague Professor Dina Stein, who was the first to see this book in its initial stages and encouraged me to continue with it. Her wise comments after reading the completed manuscript contributed much to it.

Also, a tremendous contribution to the book was made by the late Professor Haya Bar-Itzhak who, sadly, passed away much too soon in October 2020. Not only being my doctoral adviser and mentor, she was also and foremost a friend and a colleague for over forty years. She served as the academic head of IFA (1995–2014), supporting and advancing the digitization of the archives' collection. She read the manuscript several times at its various stages, offering important and enlightening insights and comments that helped immensely to complete it.

I am especially indebted to Professor Dan Ben-Amos, for his initiative and encouragement to publish the English version of this book, and his support in overcoming the hurdles encountered in the process.

I would like to thank the manuscript reviewers for their enlightening comments and important suggestions, which surely improved the book. Special thanks to the editorial board of Wayne State University Press; Kathryn Wildfong, former director; Stephanie L. Williams, the current director; Annie Martin, editor-in-chief; Marie Sweetman, acquisitions editor, who with courtesy and dedication accompanied the process in its first steps; Kristin Harpster, editorial, design, and production manager; Emily Nowak, marketing and sales manager; Kristina Stonehill, promotions manager; and Amy Pattullo, copyeditor. Thank you all for your seriousness, dedication, and professionalism.

Special thanks to Professor Barbara Kirshenblatt-Gimblett, who with remarkable courtesy and generosity provided the cover image, painted by her father.

A final thanks to Paul Ginsberg, my husband, who for years has accompanied me in the pleasure of cooking and eating, and who patiently read and commented on the English version.

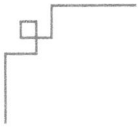

I

WORLDLY PLEASURE

FOOD AND TASTE

O ne of the earliest sensory experiences in a person's life relates to food. The first milk it suckles introduces a newborn baby to the appeasing and soothing pleasure of warm milk. The delicate and sweet taste of this first food is deeply rooted in the sensual and emotional memory of any human being.

Over the course of a lifetime, a person has a wide spectrum of sensory encounters with food: its appearance, smell, taste, texture, and the sounds attached to it. First among these is flavor. The predilection for some flavors is universal, like the taste of honey—evidence of honey collection can be found on mural paintings from the late Paleolithic period (15,000 BCE) in three continents: Africa, Europe, and Asia (Crane 1999, 36–37)—and salt (although not widespread during antiquity, it was a commodity in demand, often more valuable than gold). In ancient Egypt there is evidence of salt production from seawater as early as 1450 BCE (Marks 2010, 522).

Other tastes are acquired, subjective, or unique to a society (Montanari 2006), such as the flavor of insects or reptiles. In spite of the different and various flavors unique to each group, all human beings share the same sensual and direct enjoyment from food (Westenhoefer and Pudel 1993, 246–47; Desmet and Schifferstein 2008, 294; Bourdieu 1984). There are instances when taste is defined by the ruling class. The elite determine what is a refined taste, based on what they are able to afford, versus a poor taste, what the inferior class can obtain (Bourdieu 1984).

The pleasure from food sometimes follows people to their final days. A common custom today is to serve a last meal to persons condemned to death, so they will leave this world with the taste of their preferred meal still in their mouth.

In Jewish culture, the importance of the sensory experience of food is established in the foundational texts. The first reference to food in the Bible is to the forbidden fruit (Genesis 3:6): which was "good for food" and "pleasant to the eyes." A midrash dating from the fifth century CE comments on this verse describing the sensory experience that this fruit arouses through its flavor and its sight: "Good for food means tasty" and "Pleasant to the eyes means beautiful" (Bereshit Rabbah 19:7).

Other ancient Jewish sources mention additional flavors described as marvelous: the fruits of the tree of life in Paradise, each one of them having a particular fragrance and appearance (Eisenstein 1969, vol. 1, 84); and the manna that rained down on the Israelites in the desert (Exodus 16:1–18). According to talmudic references, the manna's flavor suited every single person: young men tasted it as bread, the elderly as honey cake, infants as mother's milk, and the sick as flour mixed with honey (Babylonian Talmud, Yoma 75a; Shemot Rabbah 5:9). Other sources mention the delicacies served to the righteous person who arrives in heaven after his death, when sixty thousand angels invite him to eat honey and drink wine reserved from the days of the creation (Eisenstein 1969, vol. 1, 83–84), and the special banquet reserved for the righteous in the days to come, where meat of legendary animals will be served (Babylonian Talmud, Baba Batra 75a; Tanhuma Shemini 7; Vayikra Rabba, Ahrey Mot 22).

These traditions are not represented in the folktales selected for this chapter, but they did penetrate folk literature, and echoes can be heard in other tales from the IFA. For example, the delicious food and wine served in Paradise are depicted: "In Paradise, a table was set, with freshly baked bread and plenty of food" (in the tale "A Burned Pita as Charity," IFA 11097, told by Dina Elazar from Turkey, and recorded by Rachel Sari) or, the marvelous taste of wine described as a "taste of Paradise" (in the tale "The Blessing of Elijah the Prophet on Yom Kippur Eve," IFA 960, recorded by Devorah Foss from her Lithuanian-born mother).[1]

Unlike Christianity, which deplores gluttony—the excessive indulgence in food and drink—as one of the seven deadly sins (Delany 1909), in Judaism the issue is more ambiguous. Nowhere in the Torah is gluttony explicitly prohibited. Some postbiblical sources condemn gluttony (Babylonian Talmud, Sanhedrin 63a; Maimonides, *Mishneh Torah*, Hilhot De'a, 4:19), while commenting on various biblical verses: "The righteous eateth to the satisfying of his soul: but the belly of the wicked shall want" (Proverbs 13:25); "Ye shall not eat any thing with the blood" (Leviticus 19:26); "But Jeshurun waxed fat, and kicked: thou art waxen fat, thou art grown thick, thou art covered with fatness; then he forsook God which made him, and lightly esteemed the Rock of his salvation" (Deuteronomy 32:15). Nevertheless, the common opinion calls for moderation while eating and drinking and denounces asceticism.

Folktales referring to the taste of food reflect the Jewish cultural reality: its respect for fine and flavorful food, the important occasions on which food is served, the pleasure derived from food, and the enjoyment of the eating experience itself. In folktales, the pleasure derived from eating one's favorite delights is appreciated, but gratification from eating, often connected to erotic feelings, raises ambivalence and is condemned.

Gluttony is engraved in human memory through narratives with a clear and unequivocal message. In the scroll of Esther, for example, banquets in the Persian monarch's court lead toward promiscuity (Esther 1: 3–11). One of the symbols of decadence and social decay is the Roman banquet, in which the participants were addicted to intemperate eating. For example, the description of such a banquet by the Roman philosopher Lucius Annaeus Seneca (4 BCE–65 CE): "The master eats more than he can hold, and with monstrous greed loads his belly until it is stretched and at length ceases to do the work of a belly; so that he is at greater pains to discharge

---

1 For a detailed discussion of this tale see Ben-Amos 2006–11, 2:105–8.

all the food than he was to stuff it down. When we recline at a banquet, one slave mops up the disgorged food, another crouches beneath the table and gathers up the left-overs of the tipsy guests" (Seneca 1917–25). In our day, various narratives examine the boundaries between pure pleasure from mouthwatering food, gluttony, and the addiction to sensual gratification. There are film treatments of, for example, obsessive eating until death occurs,[2] total devotion to taste and food texture,[3] and the consequences of eating delicacies in a puritanical society leading to loss of control and the release of latent urges.[4]

This chapter presents six folktales, three of which are concerned with foods' taste and three of which deal with gluttony and overeating. Surprisingly, not every tale condemns these debaucheries.

---

2 The French movie *La grande bouffe* (Marco Ferreri, 1973).
3 The Japanese movie *Tampopo* (Juzo Itami, 1985).
4 The Danish movie *Babettes Gaestebud* (Gabriel Axel, 1987).

THE REBBE AND WORLDLY PLEASURES

IFA 16176

TOLD BY ALEXANDER ANDZEL, POLAND
RECORDED BY AVRAHAM KEREN

A father tells his son: "Dear son, I am going away to visit the Rebbe; come with me this time for the holiday. You will see the behavior of the Hassidim near the *tish*. It is something worth seeing, it is interesting."

The son didn't really want to, but he joined his father anyway. He arrived and registered at the inn. This was on the eve of Rosh Hashanah. They went to pray. After prayers, the Rebbe performed the *Kiddush*. For the *Kiddush* they brought in the Rebbe's wife to hear it. The son sees the wife—a gorgeous woman, a stunning beauty. After the *Kiddush*, she left with her help and the Rebbe started conducting the *tish*.

Later, they brought the fish. The Rebbe takes salt and sprinkles it on the fish.

The son said: "Father, father, the Rebbe is spoiling the fish?" (He was used to eating sweet fish).

The father said: "No, no, Son. The Rebbe doesn't want to enjoy this world."

They bring in the soup, same story. He takes salt and sprinkles it on the soup. And so on with the noodles, with the meat and with the compote. He did so with everything.

For the Blessing over the food, the Rebbe's wife came in again. The son said: "Father, how much salt does the Rebbe sprinkle on her, so he won't have pleasure?"

Discussion of
"The Rebbe and Worldly Pleasures"

The storyteller, Alexander Andzel, was born in Klobuck, Poland, a town situated about 290 km southwest of Warsaw: 50°54′N, 18°56′E. Twenty-six of his tales, told in Yiddish, are registered with the IFA. This tale was filed in the archives in 1987.

This tale is a humoristic anecdote. There is an international tale type, according to the Aarne and Thompson classification (Aarne 1964) and Uther's update (Uther 2004), that is slightly similar to the oversalting tale's motif:[1]

> ATU 1328A* Oversalting the Soup. Each member of the family puts salt into the soup not knowing that it has already been salted.
> AT 1328A* Oversalting the Soup. Each member of the family remembers to put in salt.

In the international tale type, oversalting is unintentional, having been caused as each member of the family adds salt to the soup, unaware that it has already been salted. In the present tale, the oversalting is intentional, and is a result of a particular worldview. In addition, the plot of this tale

---

1 The Aarne-Thompson tale type index is a listing identifying recurring plot patterns in traditional folktales. A first index was published by Antti Aarne in 1910. This was translated, revised, and enlarged by Stith Thompson in 1928 and again in 1961. The AT-number system was updated and expanded by Hans-Jörg Uther in *The Types of International Folktales: A Classification and Bibliography* (2004). (*World Heritage Encyclopedia*, http://self.gutenberg.org/articles/aarne-thompson_classification_system).

differs from the international type and cannot be attributed to it, for the tale is rooted in the Jewish way of life.

There are two additional versions of this tale in IFA, both from Poland: the first tale, "Why the Opposer Worried about Salt Being Used Up" (IFA 4470), told by Yehiel Yeuday and recorded by Nehamat Zion; and, the second tale, "The Rebbe Should Not Enjoy Life" (IFA 14249), told by Mordechai Hillel Kroshnitz and recorded by his granddaughter Ayelet Etinger. All three of these versions describe a Hasidic gathering. In the present version, it is precisely specified: "You will see the behavior of the Hasidim near the *tish*." In another version (IFA 4470), it is mentioned as "a group of Hasidim traveled on a train to the Rabbi," and in the third version, it is said: "So a Hasid came to his Rebbe."

The framework of the plot and the time described in it are connected to the Hasidic way of life: the *tish* is a ceremonial meal offered by the rebbe in his court on Shabbat and festivals to his Hasidic followers.[2] During this meal, the Hasidim observe the Rebbe's actions and listen to his sermons. This is a Hasidic custom (Jacobs 1979, 4; Nadler 2005, 195) still in practice today. (Some of these *tish* ceremonies have been recorded and are available online.[3]) The dinner described in the tale includes dishes typical to Eastern European Jewry[4]—sweet fish, soup, noodles called *lokshen*, meat, and compote.[5]

---

2 For further reading about the *tish*, its origins, and its central place in Hasidic ritual, see Nadler 2005, 195; Jochnowitz 2015, 310.

3 The *tish* of the Rabbi of Satmer, from the Vizhnitz Hasidic dynasty, during Sukkot, recorded by Yaacov Lederman in Bnei Brak, Israel, 2011: YouTube, https://www.youtube.com/watch?v=Rc196LIDw80. The *tish* of the Belz Hasidim on Purim 2010, recorded by Yaacov Lederman: YouTube, https://www.youtube.com/watch?v=T7bBaVuwMdE. The *tish* of the Kaliver Rebbe, in Jerusalem, spring 2011: YouTube, https://www.youtube.com/watch?v=154aM37RghI.

4 For a detailed description of Eastern European Jewish cuisine see Roden 1999a, 41–57.

5 The Yiddish term *lokshen* may actually have a Persian origin in *lakhsha* which means "to slide." The noodles originated in China, and in the Middle Ages reached Europe via the Silk Road (Marks 2010, 367, "Lokshen").

The Rebbe oversalts the dishes served to him to prevent himself from attaining pleasure from eating. His deeds do not fit the Hasidic worldview, for consciously spoiling food is not present in Hasidism and is in fact the opposite.

The Hasidic movement adopted and extended a pantheistic view of deity. According to it, holiness exists and is embedded in the profane world. Holiness is achieved not only through meditation, reflection, and religious deeds, but also through mundane and daily activities, for example the act of eating (Jacobs 1979; Kauffman 2009, 282). This central principle is called within Hasidism *avodah be-gashmiyut*, "worship by substantiality," meaning "giving a religious value to actions which are not within normative religious doing" (Kauffman 2009, 282). Sensory pleasure in general, and specifically that derived from eating, is important and has a symbolic, mystical quality attributed to it (Jacobs 1979).

Indeed, in Hasidic teachings, some rabbis called on people to abstain from sinking into this pleasure, but their intention was to reduce eating, not to spoil food on purpose. For example, R. Nahman from Breslov demands: "The Righteous should eat until satiation" (*Likutei Moharan*, par. 47). But he himself did not renounce the pleasure of tasty foods and saw a holy blessing in it: "The one who cannot feel taste in his eating, should know that God has separated himself from him" (*Sefer Hamidot*, part 2, par. 6).

In Chabad Hasidism, it is told that the founder of the dynasty, Rabbi Shneor Zalman, ate a very salty dish but did not sense its taste. The first part of the tale describes how the food got too salty: his daughter prepared the dish, then his wife, the mother, added salt as a habit. This part resembles the international tale type ATU 1328*, but the rest of the tale has a Hasidic context. The explanation provided in this particular tale is that after Shneor met the *maggid* of Mezritch, his master, he lost his sense of taste. In the various versions of this tale,[6] no reason is actually provided for the meaning

---

6 Other versions of the tale can be found at the Chabad website, https://www .chabad.org.

of his loss of taste, therefore it invites one's own explanation. It may be that the studies with his teacher were so overwhelming that he disconnected himself from the earthly life, and its expression was the loss of taste.

Back to our tale, the plot describes a cultural space taken from the Hasidic world and seems to be similar to a Hasidic tale, but its message differs from the international tale type and from the Chabad Hasidic tale. Its plot is founded on an intergenerational conflict between a father and his son: the father an enthusiastic follower of the Rebbe, and his son who does not share his father's admiration. The father represents total acceptance of the rabbi's ascetic behavior and his objection to worldly pleasures. The son questions it, and points at the ridiculous and absurd sides of his father's attitude.

It may be that the son represents the storyteller's worldview, who left the Diaspora and lives now in Israel, maybe as a secular Jew. This worldview seeks to shake off the old Jewish world of Eastern Europe and its ethics.[7] The tale raises the issue of hypocrisy, the contradiction and the ludicrousness in the will to live and to spoil pleasure on purpose, in order to live allegedly in a more "ethical" way. This criticism also expresses the tension between the Rebbe and his followers, a tension that the humoristic genre enables it to express (Meyer 2000; Oring 1992). A criticism of asceticism is well conveyed through the food imagery. Any listener to the tale has experienced the taste of an oversalted dish and therefore understands the nature of such a radical and illogical, self-righteous act.

At the end of the tale, the son points out the hypocrisy of the self-righteous Rebbe, when he creates an analogy between the pleasure from food and erotic pleasure. His question—How much salt does the Rebbe need to prevent the pleasure he may have from his beautiful wife?—exposes the understood fact that here is an indulgence the Rebbe does not abstain from at all.

---

7 For the continuation of Jewish ethics and its transit from Eastern Europe to Israel in the twentieth century, see Dan 1975, 265.

LOVE LIKE SALT

IFA 5691

TOLD BY SERL HAIMOVITS, POLAND
RECORDED BY ZVI MOSHE HAIMOVITS

A king had three talented daughters whom he loved very much. However, the youngest, who was brighter and more intelligent than her sisters, he loved the most.

Would it be surprising that it aroused the jealousy of her sisters? They looked for an opportunity to take revenge against their younger sister. It arrived when the king, who wasn't that bright himself, asked his daughters how much they loved him.

The oldest daughter said: "I love you, Father, like a beautiful diamond."

The second daughter said: "I love you, Father, like the pearl necklace on my neck."

And the youngest daughter said: "I love you, Father, like salt."

The king paled. The two sisters immediately seized the opportunity and started to incite him against his youngest daughter, the ungrateful one.

The king ordered to throw her in jail.

When this was known to the queen, she sneaked into the jail and told her daughter: "You, who are so smart and wise, why did you tell the king such nonsense?"

"No Mother, this is not nonsense. Furthermore, go home, convince the king to put on a big banquet. Have him invite important guests. The head chef should prepare tasty dishes, but make sure he will cook them this time without any salt and that is how he should serve the dishes to the guests. And then we'll see what happens."

The queen did just that. While the food was being served, the diners swallowed a few spoonfuls to be polite, but they did not eat any more. The

King saw that, called in the head chef, and scolded him: "How dare you shame me? Do you know what will happen to you?"

"Yes, your Majesty," said the head chef, "but I am not to be blamed. The queen ordered me to do so, and I, your servant, followed the order."

The queen did not wait for the king to confront her and she said: "Yes, my Lord. The cook is not to be blamed. Following the advice of our wise daughter, I told the cook not to add salt to the dishes."

The king understood that there is no substitute for salt. It cannot be replaced by a diamond or any other expensive item in the world. If you are missing salt, you miss everything. The king accepted that it is so, and released his young daughter from jail.

Discussion of
"LOVE LIKE SALT"

This tale was told by Serl Haimovits, who was born in 1905 in Mogielnica, Poland, a town situated about 70 km southwest of Warsaw: 51°41′23″N, 20°43′23″E. She immigrated to Israel in 1932. Her husband, Zvi Moshe Haimovits, recorded her tales, twenty-nine of which are registered at IFA. She heard them in her childhood at home from her mother. This tale was filed in the archives in 1963.

The tale "Love Like Salt" matches the international tale type classified by Hans-Jorg Uther as ATU 923, Love Like Salt. In tales of this type, a king (a rich man) asks his three daughters how much they love him. The two elder ones compare their love with precious (sweet) things (gold, precious stones, sugar, honey, luxurious clothes), but the youngest says that she loves him like salt (according to Stith Thompson motif index classification H592.1: Thompson 1955). The father is offended by his youngest daughter's answer and casts her out (orders her death), whereas he rewards the elder daughters in proportion to the value of their flatteries (according to Thompson motif index classification M21). The youngest daughter then works as a maidservant in a foreign country whose king she later marries. She invites her father to the wedding meal and serves him dishes without any salt. Thus, the father becomes aware of the indispensability of salt. The daughter then discloses her identity (Uther 2004, 555).

Versions of this type date from the Middle Ages and are widespread in fifty countries stretching across four continents (Uther 2004, 555–56). In the Israel Folktale Archives sixteen versions of this tale are registered. They were recorded during a period of time stretching from the foundation of IFA up to the present.[1] The multiple versions of the tale, their dispersal around the world, and the fact that it has been told over the centuries point to its relevance and importance to humanity.

Across the numerous versions the older sisters compare their love for their father to a variety of items. In some these are precious objects such as gold, silver, and diamonds. In others they are sweets, such as sugar and honey, and sometimes they are celestial objects such as the sun and the moon. The youngest daughter's answer, though, is constant. In all the tale's versions, her love is compared to salt.

The exposition of our tale is tainted with an incestuous insinuation: the father's intense love for his youngest daughter, the jealousy of the elder sisters, and his demand to know the extent of his daughters' love for him. Some scholars have already discussed this point (Alexander 2008, 244). Alan Dundes, in his article about Shakespeare's *King Lear*, discussed the projection of the daughter yearning for her father and the reversed sexual tension between father and daughter (Dundes 1983).

Salt is a crucial element for human existence and for centuries has been an important factor in society and its economy (Kurlansky 2002). Numerous researches point at the extended symbolism of salt. Some researchers have noted the similarity between the meanings given to salt and those given to semen (E. Jones 1923; Alexander 2008, 377). This specific meaning of salt intensifies the incestuous dimension in the tale and fits within

---

1 The versions registered in IFA are: one tale from Afghanistan, IFA 5225; one tale from Greece, IFA 21635 (the daughter marries a prince immediately after being expelled from the palace by her father, who ordered her to be killed); six tales from Iraq: IFA 1665 (this is the first version of the tale recorded in IFA in the year 1959), IFA 3477, IFA 9380, IFA 12008, IFA 24032, IFA 24071 (this is the most recent version, 2010, registered in the archives); one tale from Iraqi Kurdistan, IFA 19966 (this tale is between a father and his sons, and the youngest one cooks without salt); two tales from Morocco, IFA 14896 and IFA 23396; one tale from Persia, IFA 4492 (there the children are two sons and a daughter); one tale from Romania, IFA 5956; one tale from Russia, IFA 8002; and one tale from Turkey, IFA 16575.

some folktale genres, for example, the fairytale in which a social taboo is broken and even legitimized (Bar-Itzhak 1993; Milo 2008).

At the tale's opening, it seems that the comparison between "fatherly love" and "salt love" is inappropriate. While each of the older daughters refers to their love for their father as to a precious object, the youngest daughter compares hers to salt. Although at times in the past salt was considered a precious and expensive item (Kurlansky 2002), it is not the case in this tale. The angry and offended father seems to view salt as a cheap, easily available, common commodity.

This tale emphasizes that the daughter appears more intelligent than her father. This may even be the reason he prefers her to his other daughters, hinting that her answer may have a deeper meaning than at first appears. This concealed significance is hidden to the loving father and even to the supportive mother, as well as to the jealous sisters who try to denigrate her in their father's eyes. The mother acknowledges that there must be a reason for the daughter's answer but cannot understand it and considers it nonsense.

The young daughter is punished for her answer and sent to jail. This pause is a kind of liminal stage in which she suffers humiliation and banishment, but is a necessary step to ensure the proper functioning of the family system.

The young daughter sends her mother to provide food for the father, and asks her to do so in public, in front of numerous guests. In doing so, the mother—the king's wife—enters the picture in the position of a spouse. She serves food to her husband, an act that may be interpreted as proof of her love toward him. This should be considered as an act of proper love: the father, while he either does not ask for or demands it, receives confirmation of his wife's love.

However, this does not resolve everything. As per the youngest daughter's request, the mother orders the cooks to serve the king unsalted food, which the guests are unable to eat. The young daughter shows her father that there is no taste in life without salt. She appeases him and proves that her love for him is deep and cannot be compromised, as both of them need it.

However, this message could have been conveyed through other items, for example, water. Therefore the question remains: Why in all the numerous versions of the tale does the daughter compare her love specifically to salt?

The choice of salt is deliberate and necessary in order to convey yet another hidden message. It is based on a culinary fact, well known to all, that the use of salt in cooking should be done very carefully and one should be extremely precise in the amount used. There is a very narrow boundary between a dish not salted enough and one salted too much. Using this metaphor, the daughter points to the limits of love, its dangers and its correct measure–"the good taste" in its double meaning—between a father and his daughter. The daughter indicates the desirable boundaries of love and in doing so she restores the relations between her and her father to the appropriate status and rehabilitates their family ties. Scholars have previously mentioned the affinity between this tale and *King Lear* (Dundes 1983; Rush 1994, 201). There, Cordelia, the king's youngest daughter, describes the proper dimensions of a daughter's love for her father: "I love your majesty according to my bond; nor more nor less. . . . Haply, when I shall wed, that lord whose hand must take my plight shall carry half my love with him, half my care and duty: sure, I shall never marry like my sisters, to love my father all" (act 1, scene 1).

The proposed solution is understood intuitively. It is based on a direct and common knowledge of the taste of salt and on the subtle limits between tasty saltiness and excessive saltiness, which turns food into something inedible—the same limit existing between proper and exaggerated love. "Love Like Salt" is the proper love between daughter and father, no less and no more. It is now possible to understand the relevance of the tale to any society, because it concerns a sensitive and universal issue.

HOME-COOKED FOOD

IFA 14221

TOLD BY MORDECHAI HILLEL KROSHNITZ, POLAND
RECORDED BY AYELET ETINGER

A Jewish man, whose wife traveled for a long period, some three or four months overseas, was eating in restaurants.

One day he enters a restaurant and tells the waiter: "Maybe you have some soup from yesterday, a little sour, in a plate stained with sooty fingerprints"?

The waiter goes into the kitchen and asks the cook: "Do we have such a thing?"

The cook replies: "Yes, we have leftover soup from yesterday, there. We wanted to leave it for the dog, for it is sour already."

The waiter says: "Good, prepare a serving."

He ladled it into a soup bowl, took some soot from under the pots and served it to the Jewish man.

The Jewish man ate it and said: "Ah, it's tasty, so tasty, it's good!"

Then he says: "Bring me some meat for the second course. The meat should smell a little, and be burned on top, with a little bit of hair."

The waiter enters the kitchen and says: "What a nut case—but, he is the customer. What can you do?"

The cook says: "Over there is some meat, left for the dog and the cats. The meat is from yesterday, it's summer, and it smells already."

The waiter took it, pulled some hair from the female cook and placed them on it, put it on the fire to burn it a little and brought it to him.

The Jewish man eats the meat and then says: "Bring me some compote, sour as vinegar, sour."

So, the waiter enters the kitchen, takes the compote, pours some vinegar on it, puts lemon—what do I know, vinegar—and brings it to him.

The Jewish man finishes eating, and asks the waiter: "How much do I owe you for this lunch?"

The waiter says: "I'll tell you the truth mister, for a good lunch we take ten lira. But for that, I don't know how to calculate. Give me as much as you think."

He says: "No, no, no." He takes out ten lira, gives it to him, and adds two more as a tip.

Then the waiter says: "Sir, I would like to ask you a question."

He says: "Ask."

"Look, I thought you didn't have any money, or you were a miser. But with your money you could have bought yourself a nice lunch, fresh, tasty. Why did you need all this?"

"Listen, my wife is overseas three months already. I was craving a home-cooked meal, a lunch like at home. I was craving home-cooked food."

Discussion of
"HOME-COOKED FOOD"

Mordechai Hillel Kroshnitz, the storyteller, was born in 1915 in Baranavicze, Poland, today in Belarus, 53°08′N, 26°01′E. He immigrated to Israel in 1949. His mostly humoristic tales were told to his granddaughter Ayelet Etinger, who recorded them and gave two hundred of them to IFA. This tale was filed in the archives in 1983.

This humorous tale raises the question of the subjectivity of food's taste, and discusses in an implied way the emotional connection to food and its reflection on a couple's intimacy.

The tale's opening displays a situation of absence: the wife is missing from home for a very long time, so her husband goes out to eat in restaurants. The audience listening may assume that this man was used to tasty home-cooked food prepared by his wife. During her absence, he looks for a suitable substitute in restaurants. We expect that for a fair amount of money he will be served in a restaurant the freshest and tastiest food, closest in quality to the food he is used to being served at home. Surprisingly, the man himself asks for what is inappropriate food.[1] It is inappropriate for the following reasons:

The food is not cooked properly and is burned
The food is not fresh; it is spoiled, almost rotten[2]

---

1 See the model suggested by David Navon, and the stage he calls "inadequate" (Navon 1981).

2 Lévi-Strauss discusses the subjective aspect of the definition of rotten food, because in certain cultures some food goes through a fermentation process, e.g., French cheese: "Rotting, too, is only allowed to take place in certain specific

The food is not clean, it has hair on it
The food is served in dirty dishes, stained with sooty fingerprints
The food is not tasty, it is too sour

The tale emphasizes that this kind of food is not appropriate for human consumption, and twice mentions that it is intended for cats and dogs. Furthermore, at the end of the tale the waiter does not know what to charge for such a meal. He is convinced that the real reason the man asks for such poor quality food is because either he is a miser or he is poor.

According to the man's answer, the reason for his peculiar requests is revealed: he is longing for a "home-cooked meal" like his wife used to prepare for him.

Based only on the plot, it is not possible to determine why his wife was serving him such spoiled food. Is it for lack of training, negligence, or from malice? The wife's absence from home during a few months may represent her failure to function as a proper spouse, who is supposed to feed her husband with high-quality food, according to the norms of the society telling the tale.

The impropriety of this couple's relationship includes a humorous element: the ridiculous and ludicrous acceptance on the part of the husband of his humiliating situation, and his desire to maintain it by ordering food just like it in a restaurant. The comic dimension in the insistence on repeating the same situation, although it cannot reverse itself, fits the principle of "repetitive mechanism" identified by Henri Bergson (Bergson 1983, 63–68). In David Navon's models, this principle is called "inadequate resolution" (Navon 1981). The absurdity of the husband's acts is emphasized by the fact that he discloses his situation in public and shares with the

ways, either spontaneous or controlled" (Lévi-Strauss 1997, 29). Nevertheless, it is clear that in our tale the narrator and his audience see the inappropriate dishes as truly spoiled.

waiter, and with all of us, details about the kind of food he eats at home. In other words, he exposes his intimacy with his wife.

The humor of the tale enables a society to cope with a painful issue,[3] apparently private, of an unfit marriage. The ridiculousness of the inappropriate situation leads to an understanding of the desirable situation and appropriate gender functions.

---

3 On the social functions of humor, see Meyer 2000.

Who Will Be the Baal Shem Tov's Neighbor in the World to Come?

IFA 9127

Told by Malka Herts, Ukraine
Recorded by Yifrah Haviv

The Baal Shem Tov wanted to know who will be his neighbor in the World to Come. He went to a rabbi and told him about it. The rabbi gave him a certain address and said: "Travel and keep on traveling. You will exit the boundary of the town. Travel a bit further until you see a large forest. Turn and keep turning, and when you come to the forest's edge you will see a big forge. The blacksmith working there is your neighbor in the World to Come."

The Baal Shem Tov followed the rabbi's instructions, rented a cart, and traveled. When he got to the forest's edge, he found the blacksmith shop and the smith—huge, fat, hulking, dirty, dark as coal—standing and working.

The Baal Shem Tov stood in front of him and stared at him. He thought to himself: I will stay here the whole day and see how he works and lives his day-to-day life.

The Baal Shem Tov sat in the shade of a tree and watched. The time for *Shacharit*, the morning prayer, arrived. The blacksmith, without washing his hands and without blessing his bread and food, sat and ate, gobbling and devouring it like a wild animal.

Some hours passed. It was noon and the same scene repeated itself. The blacksmith sat down without washing his hands and without blessing the food and bread, and devoured and gulped like a machine for a full hour. The grinding of his teeth could be heard from afar. When it was time for *Mincha*, the afternoon prayer, the Baal Shem Tov waited and observed, and once again, it was the same show. In the evening, the blacksmith did not wash his hands, did not bless the bread but chewed and chewed endlessly.

The Baal Shem Tov thought to himself: This will be my neighbor in the World to Come?

He asked the blacksmith: "Can I stay here for the night?"

The blacksmith answered: "There is straw on the ground, it is where I sleep. There will be room for you too."

The Baal Shem Tov went to the blacksmith's hut, sat on the straw, and decided to himself: I am going to ask him to explain his behavior to me. I will talk to him so I will know why he is acting this way.

He opened his mouth and told the blacksmith: "Answer me sir. I have a question for you. Tell me how a Jewish person can eat and gulp so much?"

The blacksmith answered him: "Do you really want to know? I'll tell you. My father was a peddler and used to wander with his merchandise on roads and in villages. He was small, thin as a raisin, a pious man, always reciting a blessing, mumbling a prayer. Nevertheless, it did not prevent his bitter fate. One day, rioters caught him and burned him at the stake. And this is what the neighbors told me: 'A small fire came from your father while he was in flames. And the bonfire extinguished promptly'.

"Back then, I was only a child but the life story of my father I took to heart and decided: I will be big and strong, very strong! And, when the rioters will catch me and will want to kill and burn me, an immense flame will come out of me. And this bonfire will say: Not easily a Jew is burnt! And this huge fire will consume his rioters as well."

After the Baal Shem Tov heard this, he decided: "I am glad to have found this Jewish man and to have him as my neighbor in the World to Come."

"Who Will Be the Baal Shem Tov's Neighbor in the World to Come?"

Malka Herts, the storyteller, was born in 1903 in Yaryshiv, situated in the southwest of Ukraine: 48°32″N, 27°38″E. She immigrated to Israel in 1923. Five of her tales are registered at IFA and were recorded by her nephew, Yifrah Haviv. This tale was filed in the archives in 1971.

This tale is attributed to the oicotype AT 809*-*A (IFA), the Companion in Paradise. This oicotype is composed of numerous plot parts, therefore various versions of the tale differ considerably from one another.

The structure of the oicotype is:

I. Rabbi wants to know who will be his neighbor in Paradise.

II. Rabbi is answered.

 A. He is answered: 1) in a dream (by an angel or by Elijah the Prophet); 2) by a heavenly voice.

 B. His neighbor will be a seemingly evil person, who does not observe religious laws: 1) a butcher; 2) a stingy rich man; 3) a water carrier; 4) a smith.

III. Rabbi seeks to know why a seemingly undeserving person is destined to be his neighbor in Paradise:

 A. 1) For ransoming a Jewish girl, intending to marry her to his only son, but when learning at the wedding that she was betrothed to another man present at the ceremony, giving her to the latter;

2) for ransoming a group of captive Jewish boys and girls and marrying them to each other.

B. For giving charity in secret: 1) meat to the poor for Shabbat; 2) helping the poor to marry their children.

C. For resolving to become big and strong, so that when he will be burned at the stake, his body will fuel a huge fire.

In IFA, there are twenty-three tales registered under this oicotype and it is still told to this day.[1] Ancient versions are also found in Jewish sources.[2]

The tale presented here is composed of the following oicotype parts: AT 809*-*A I, IIB4, IIIC.

I. Rabbi wants to know who will be his neighbor in Paradise.

IIB4. His neighbor will be a smith.

IIIC. Smith has resolved to become big and strong so that, when he will be burned at the stake, his body will fuel a huge fire.

Three other versions paralleling our tale are registered in IFA.[3] Tamar Alexander researched the pattern common to the oicotype, and discerned three parts: 1) the worldly inquiry and its heavenly answer; 2) the quest and the meeting; and 3) the recognition. Alexander describes the process occurring in these parts:

---

1 For a short survey of these tales see Ben-Amos 2006–11, 1:206–7.

2 For more details on the ancient versions see Alexander 1981, 65–66 and Ben-Amos 2006–11, 1:202–7.

3 "The Baal Shem Tov Visits Shmerl the Smith" (IFA 13136), told by Pinhas Shteinfeld from Lithuania and recorded by Malka Cohen; "Kiddush Hashem" [The sanctification of God's name through martyrdom] (IFA 14610), told by Aharon Ben Dov from Czech Republic and recorded by Yonit Barak; "Neighbor in Paradise" (IFA 15949), told by Tova Haberman from Poland and recorded by Adina Bar-Ilan. A version of this tale was adapted for the stage in the play "Once There Was a Hassid" by Dan Almagor in 1968 and was performed by the troupe BIMOT.

A person of a high religious status (such as a rabbi, a righteous person, or a religious scholar) wants to know what will be his reward in the world to come. The heavenly answer is that someone inferior to him (a butcher, a cook) will be rewarded, as he will. The allegedly perfect person is annoyed and goes to look for his inferior colleague. As a result of his inquiry, the simple person tells him about a unique moral deed he performed (such as giving charity, freeing a captive), the high religious status's person recognizes the justified heavenly judgment. (Alexander 1981, 65–66)

Our tale, in its structure, resembles the pattern formulated by Alexander but differs from it, first of all, in its realism. The Baal Shem Tov does not direct his request to heaven but to another rabbi. The differences increase as the plot evolves. For example, at the beginning of our tale the Baal Shem Tov, who himself has a high religious status, turns to another rabbi as if he himself were a common person.[4] The rabbi refers him to a smith offering no explanation as to how he happened to know that he will be his neighbor in the world to come. An additional prominent and significant difference is the reason given for the future neighboring of these two characters in Paradise. In the general oicotype, a common person performs an outstanding or hidden moral act. In our tale, it seems at first that gluttony lacks a moral aspect, although some scholars saw it as a kind of *avodah begashmiut* (worship by substantiality),[5] according to Hasidic ethics (Bar-Itzhak 1987, 104).

The question opening the tale is based on the belief that a righteous person is entitled to enter Paradise after his death. Paradise's common description in Jewish sources is of a Torah academy, where scholars sit according

---

4 About the centrality of the Baal Shem Tov in Jewish Folklore see Bar-Itzhak 1987; Patai and Sebba-Elran 2013.

5 See discussion of this chapter's first tale, "The Rebbe and Worldly Pleasures" (IFA 16176).

to their erudition.[6] Therefore, people sitting next to each other should be of an equivalent status. The implied message conveyed by the question is where this person will be seated, or in other words, what type of compensation and appreciation he should get in the world to come. An answer to this question should become clear to him if the acts he performed in this world are proper.

The surprise, and maybe the disappointment, is to discover that the neighbor is an apparently unworthy person. Tamar Alexander points to the subversive character of this part of the plot: "Actually, God's judgment is questioned, the protagonist doubts the promised reward to his deeds, for an inferior person receives the same reward" (Alexander 1981, 66).

In our tale, the neighbor is an obese and rude person who does not perform the mitzvahs of washing one's hands and making the blessing over food, and who gorges himself. A turning point in the plot occurs when the aim for eating and its nature are revealed. Unexpectedly, the motive of the smith is not gluttony and shameless unrestraint, but is a conscious and deliberate act whose goal is to obtain physical, bodily presence. His objective is to ensure that his fate will differ from that of his father's who was abused, set on fire, and consumed in a small flame. The smith seeks to develop a huge body so his existence will be noticeable through an extended death and enormous flames; flames that may burn his aggressors too. His readiness to die an excruciating death, if needed, ensures him an honorable place in the world to come.

The smith's willingness to die at the stake connotes the tale about Rabbi Haninah ben Tardiyon's death—one of the ten martyrs executed by the Romans, who died at the stake wrapped in a Torah scroll (Babylonian Talmud, Avodah Zara 18a). Contemporarily, our tale is told in the context of the Holocaust. This connection is present in popular consciousness, where a subtle allusion to the extermination camps' crematoria is present. Dan

---

6 See such a description in Eisenstein 1969, 1:84.

Almagor's adaptation of the tale to a theatrical play, *Once There Was a Hassid* (the Broadway show title was *Only Fools Are Sad*), is an example.[7]

In this context, the tale can be seen as an intergenerational dialogue between the father's generation, Jews who perished in the Holocaust, and the son's generation, who represent the Zionist movement since the State of Israel's establishment. The tiny father symbolizes Jews who lived in the pre–World War II Diaspora. He lacks physical presence, lives modestly, almost ascetically, seeking to suppress his existence as if to erase it. The death of this generation is depicted through the image of the diminutive father burned at the stake, leaving no impact or memory. In contrast, the representation of the generation of sons who left their parents' way of life and intentionally chose a hedonistic lifestyle expresses their right to live and to prove it through substantial physical presence. The son does not recoil from his fate; indeed, he is ready to die a martyr's death in the name of his Jewishness. The difference between him and his father is in his physical existence, represented here by the immense flames that will arise from his bodily fats. This is a powerful, macabre scene whose meaning is but one: it is surely impossible to ignore the son's existence, which represents the new Jewish generation.

---

7 Dan Almagor, *Ish Hassid haya*, Ben Yehuda Project, accessed January 7, 2021, https://benyehuda.org/read/11111.

Big Eyes

IFA 17230

TOLD BY PENINAH FELDMAN, ARGENTINA
RECORDED BY YIFRAH HAVIV

A poor Jewish man got to a town on Shabbat eve and approached the Jewish community.

"Who is the richest Jew in town?" he asked.

They pointed at so and so and said: "He is the richest Jew" and added, "he hosts very nicely, but he has a particular habit."

"What is it?"

"He serves only fish at his table, all different types and varieties, but just fish."

"What will be, will be," sighed the poor man.

He approached the rich man, reached out his hand to him and said: "Dear sir, I am a guest in this town, a poor man and I want to spend the Shabbat at your place. My name is so and so."

"With great delight," said the rich man, "you will be our guest of honor."

Immediately he commenced with the mitzvah of hospitality. He treated his guest with respect, as is appropriate for an honored guest on the Shabbat eve.

Then it was time for the meal. The first course was served: cooked fish. The guest ate with great gusto, waiting for the second course, and then it came: stuffed fish. The guest ate enthusiastically and waited for the third course, and here it came: fried fish. The guest ate gluttonously and waited for the fourth course: fish in sauce. The guest gorged himself, and did not miss even one type of the fish dishes served at the table. When they were done serving the fish, they started serving soup, and then chicken, and then the main course of the meal. But, the poor man's stomach was so full that he could not even taste one more dish.

The moral of the tale is: He who has big eyes, deserves such a punishment!

Discussion of
"Big Eyes"

Peninah Feldman, the storyteller, was born in 1945 in Buenos Aires. She immigrated to Israel in 1982 and lives on Kibbutz Beth Keshet. Thirty-two of her tales are registered at IFA, all of them recorded by Yifrah Haviv, a member of the same kibbutz. She tells the tales she heard from her mother. This tale was filed in the archives in 1990.

This is an anecdote of a humoristic genre. The tale is not related to any universal tale type or oicotype. In IFA, one other version of the tale is registered.[1]

This tale has a didactic tone condemning gluttony. The characters are represented in a dichotomous way: the positive character is represented by the richest Jew and the negative character is depicted as the poor man. The poor man's behavior contradicts the normative and proper ways of hospitality. He inquires to find out who is the richest person in town. It can reasonably be assumed that it is to guarantee that he will get the best accommodation and the finest food. In doing so, he hurts the feelings of the other Jews who in his eyes are not suitable to host him because of their economic situation. He also prevents them from fulfilling the mitzvah of hospitality. His improper behavior is described further as the plot develops; he is the one who demands to be hosted by the rich man and does not wait for his invitation. Even his unrestrained eating contradicts proper table manners. As opposed to him, the rich man is described in a positive light. He invites the poor person to share the Shabbat meal and treats him with respect.

---

1 The additional tale is "The Glutton Miser" (IFA 13094), told by Yizhak Hillel Cohen of Romania and recorded by Malka Cohen.

The meal is described in detail with a particular emphasis on the different fish dishes, according to the way they were prepared. This detailed description may have an artistic purpose to depict the host's generosity and the guest's gluttony and may not be based on a culinary reality,[2] for on Shabbat eve it is customary to eat only one or two fish dishes[3] (Roden 1999a: 94; Holland 2011: 116–17).

After the first course of numerous fish dishes, other tasty and diverse dishes follow. The poor man, already satiated, cannot even taste them. The tale ends with the moral that "he who has big eyes, deserves such a punishment." The audience does not need to hear this lesson. The plot is clear. The poor man's gluttony is his punishment.

---

2 On Jewish Argentinean cuisine see Laznow 2017, 2019.

3 On eating fish on Shabbat eve, see chapter 5 of this book. On the central place of fish in Jewish cuisine, see Horowitz 2014, 57–66.

Diet

IFA 4515

TOLD BY HUGO HAIM MUSTAKI, ITALY
RECORDED BY MENAHEM BEN ARIEH

A glutton used to eat a lot and gorged himself on food. In the morning, he ate twenty hard-boiled eggs, half a kilo of cheese, two loaves of bread, and drank two bottles of milk. At ten o'clock, he ate half a kilo of meat, half a kilo of tomatoes, and a kilo of apples. At noon, he ate two kilos of macaroni, two kilos of potatoes, one kilo of meat, and a kilo of bananas. At four o'clock, he drank six cups of tea, ate two loaves of bread, two packages of margarine, a jar of jam, and half a kilo of cheese. And, at eight o'clock in the evening, he ate two chickens, a kilo of fish, a kilo of potatoes, and a kilo of apples.

Once he got sick and felt pains in his stomach. He went to the doctor and complained of stomach aches. The doctor asked him what he ate. He told him and described in detail all that he ate.

The amazed doctor told the sick glutton: "If you want to be healthy, you have to eat in the morning a cup of milk and two pieces of toast. At noon, eat a plate of soup and a little piece of meat and one apple. And at eight o'clock in the evening, eat a piece of chicken, an apple and drink a cup of tea."

The glutton asked him: "Well doctor, do I have to eat that before my meals or after them?"

Discussion of
"Diet"

Biographical information on Hugo Haim Mustaki, the storyteller, are lacking at the archives. Nine tales are registered in his name in IFA. This tale was filed in the archives in 1962.

This tale describes gluttony in a humoristic way. The protagonist's body features are not mentioned, but three other elements are emphasized: the food he eats, the quantities, and his precise eating schedule. Two of these elements are realistic: the food and the eating schedule, which seems to be logical: five meals a day: three main meals at morning, noon, and evening, and two light snacks at ten and at four o'clock. The meals' components seem reasonable as well, except for the ten o'clock snack, when the protagonist eats an apple, appropriate for a light snack, but in addition he eats meat and tomatoes as well. On the other hand, the amount of food described in detail is certainly unusual: it is enormous.

The audience listening to the tale becomes aware of the unusual amounts eaten by the glutton. He is described as a kind of eating machine. This transition from the human dimension to a mechanical one elevates our laughter (Bergson 1999, 20).

On the opposite side of this tale stands the doctor. According to the plot, he is an erudite and authoritative figure. His task is to draw the glutton's attention to the proper norm in the eyes of the audience. As an authoritative figure, the doctor minutely prescribes the amount of food the glutton should eat. This amount is reasonable for one to lead a healthy way of life, or in the doctor's words, "if you want to be healthy." In saying so, the exaggerated eating is displayed. For example, he recommends drinking a glass of milk in the morning, as opposed to two bottles of milk the glutton is used to, and recommends eating two slices of toast rather than two whole loaves of bread.

The tale ends with an additional comic component—the "sting"—the term used by David Navon.[1] The humor derives from the glutton's erroneous interpretation of the doctor's prescription. The glutton understands the diet he received from the doctor to be in addition to what he is used to eating. This interpretation arouses the audience's laughter.

1 For the structure of jokes and their comic elements, see Navon 1981.

2

HE BROUGHT A
CHICKEN FOR
HER TO COOK

FOOD AND GENDER

E xamining the affinity between food and gender in folktales unveils an intricate set of meanings. Food may reflect gender identity, constituting a means for defining and strengthening it (Avakian and Haber 2005; Counihan and Kaplan 1998).[1] Food distinguishes between men and women while simultaneously serving as a communication channel between them (Gregory 1999). In addition, food may symbolize sexuality and eating represents sexual intercourse (Counihan 1999).

Food also reflects power relations between women and men and their respective roles in obtaining food, cooking it, and consuming it. The power relationship may lead to sexual equality, but may also obstruct the balance between them. For example, when men control the means of providing

---

1 Although nowadays scholars disagree on the definition of gender, in the following chapter, the term chosen for the discussion is the various attributes given to the biological sexes, originating from social and cultural conventions (Stoller 1968, 9; Butler 1990, 10).

food they can assume the mantle of food authority and judge the dishes prepared by women. In contrast, women have the power to stop cooking or, alternatively, prepare food that men loathe but have no choice but to eat (Counihan 1999).

In numerous cultures, food is a resource ruled by women and it is their duty to prepare it (Avakian 1997; Avakian and Haber 2005; Bynum 1987; Gregory 1999; Sered 1988, 1992). Gender distinction is clear: "Women cook and men eat" (Bynum 1987; Goode 1992). The reason may lie in the biological fact that a woman breastfeeds, therefore she is considered as the main supplier of nourishment essential to the next generation's survival (Bynum 1987). Women assign emotional meaning to food preparation and its delivery. A part of their gender identity and their personal definition as spouses and mothers is rooted in their ability to serve good quality food to their families and especially to their spouses (De Vault 1991). For women, food is a way to express love and care, and the satisfaction they derive from cooking depends on the pleasure food elicits in others (Charles and Kerr 1988; Avakian and Haber 2005, 264).

In traditional Jewish culture, one of the duties imposed on women was tending to food as described in the Mishnah: "These are the labors that a wife performs for her husband: *she grinds, she bakes,* she washes, *she cooks, she nurses her child,* she makes his bed, and she works in wool" (Mishnah Ketuboth 5:5, my emphasis).

In Jewish communities where men were absent from home for extended periods, either for making a livelihood or to study the Torah in distant academies, women had the obligation to stay home; they were even called "the home." In the Babylonian Talmud, this idiom appears over seventy times. Women had to supply sustenance and provide quality of life for their household (Myerhoff 1978; Sered 1992). They were required to manage their usually meager economic resources in order to purchase provisions and cook them so the food would sustain the whole family.

Another distinguishing characteristic of Jewish society is that food is an essential component of religious identity. One of the main vehicles for preserving Jewish identity is the consumption of kosher food—eating only animals allowed by the Torah and slaughtered according to Jewish law, preparing food and serving it while strictly observing the separation between milk and meat products. Furthermore, once a year on Passover women were required to provide unleavened food only, paying strict attention to the food's preparation and the purchase of appropriate products. These subjects are also reflected in folktales, as will be discussed in chapter 4. For example, in one not included here, the folktale IFA 13749, "Three Reasons to Make Life Easier," a poor woman found a wheat grain inside the turkey she purchased for Passover, and asked the rebbe in a trembling voice if it was kosher for Passover.[2]

The multiple duties of women in all matters related to food and foodways were not only a source of effort and concern, but were also a domain of control that provided women with extended power (Sered 1988, 1992). Women received a central religious stature by way of managing their kitchens, as the anthropologist Joëlle Bahloul (1983, 20–21) pointed out: "The ritualization of Jewish foodways turned the table into a reduced shrine, the kitchen into an altar . . . and the woman into a priest."

The folktales included in this chapter reflect the main themes related to food and gender: roles and gender identity, power relations between the sexes, affinity between sexuality and food, and food as a domain of a woman's authority. Deviation from the accepted gender roles leads most of the time to conflict. Generally, whoever deviates from his or her role is punished, and even dies. When both genders fail to perform according to their traditional roles they bring disaster on their home and on themselves. However, when the situation is resolved not only is the house rehabilitated but the whole society is as well.

---

2 "Three Reasons to Make Life Easier" (IFA 13749), told by Shlomo Prever, Poland, and recorded by Avraham Keren.

THE BOUNDARIES OF CRAVING

IFA 22813

TOLD AND RECORDED BY
MIRIAM AHARON AZRIEL, YEMEN

There was a man who went to the butcher every day and bought a chicken. He then brought the chicken home and handed it to his wife so she would prepare savory dishes with it. The wife labored and cooked, and at lunchtime her husband came home to eat. The good wife served the food in a large bowl and placed it on the table in front of her husband.

The husband pulled the bowl close to him and the meal began: "I will not give you the wings, so you won't fly out of the house," and he ate them. "The legs I will not give you, so you'll stay home and will not wander out into the neighbors' homes. The honor of a king's daughter is within," and he ate them. "I will not give you the head, so you will not raise yours over your husband, who is the head of all," and he ate it.

And, so it went with all the chicken's parts, until he finished eating them all and left in the bowl just their bones for his wife to clear off. This repeated itself over and over again.

One day, the wife poured out her sorrow to her neighbor. The neighbor could not bear the injustice done to her and told her, "Tomorrow, when he brings you the chicken, prepare it and eat it before he comes home. And deny that he bought it."

The following day, she acted according to her good neighbor's advice.

The husband came home at noon and waited as usual for his lunch. After some time the meal was not served, so the husband asked his wife: "Where is the cooked chicken?"

"What chicken?" replied the wife.

"The chicken I brought you this morning!" said the husband.

"Today you did not bring me any chicken!" answered the wife.

"This morning, I brought you a chicken and went back to work. Where is it?"

The wife continued to deny that he brought her a chicken and the husband got mad, yelled, and was furious. The argument heated up. The husband lost his temper and could not control himself. He was so infuriated that he had a stroke and collapsed dead.

The funeral preparations started and the entire town came to accompany him in his last journey. While following the casket, the butcher turned to the person walking by his side and told him: "Look what a world; man does not have any value. Only this morning, this man bought a chicken from me and now we are burying him."

Suddenly, the dead man awakens, sits up, and shouts to the butcher: "Right it is. I did buy a chicken from you this morning. You are my witness, tell my wife."

The people bearing the coffin ran in panic and the funeral procession scattered in all directions.

When they returned home, the couple went to a judge and he ruled how they should divide the chicken between them.

Discussion of
"THE BOUNDARIES
OF CRAVING"

Miriam Aharon Azriel, the storyteller, was born in 1947 in Erfoud, a town in southeast Morocco 31°26′10″N, 4°13′58″W. She immigrated to Israel at six months of age. During the last decades, she recorded tales that she heard from her family, many of them from her Yemenite stepfather. Twenty-three of these tales are recorded in IFA. This tale was filed in the Archives in 2004.

This tale deals with the relationship of a couple and the power struggle between the sexes. It is expressed through the description of their actions related to an unshared meal; the husband does not include his wife in eating the dishes she prepared and starves her. Food figures in this tale as a key symbol of the couple's relationship.[1] The tale opens with a description of the equilibrium existing between the two genders, allegedly an ideal situation according to the society in which the tale is told. Every day the dedicated husband brings home a chicken, considered in this society a valuable foodstuff, and gives it to his wife to prepare. The tale emphasizes the so-called good wife's actions connected to the meal: she endeavors, cooks, and serves the lunch in a "large bowl," an expression chosen by the storyteller possibly as a hint of the bounty served on the table. Up to this point, the traditional gender roles of the patriarchal society are carried out. We can assume that the described relations are proper.

---

1 A key symbol is a major component in a given culture and most significant to its settings (Ortner 1973).

The balance is breached though when the husband does not share with his wife the meal she prepared. He presents various reasons why she cannot receive any part of the chicken and finally eats it all by himself while she remains hungry. The shameful manner in which the husband treats his wife is revealed, exposing their troubled relationship.

The husband's actions are consistent with descriptions found in two separate, ancient texts.

One is a midrash from Lamentations Rabbah (1, 4)[2] and is ascribed to the international folktale type AT 1533, the Wise Carving of the Fowl,[3] in which every part of the chicken symbolizes a member of the family. A clever person divides it symbolically: head to head of house, neck to wife, wings to daughters, legs to sons, thus keeping the rest for himself.

The second text is Midrash Tanhuma (Parashat Vayeshev 6, 2) which explains why Eve was created from Adam's rib and not from another part of his body: "When God wanted to create Eve he was debating from which part he should create her. He said: If I create her from the head, she may be rude, from the eye, she may be curious, from the mouth, she may be a prattler, from the ear, she may be disobedient, from the arms, she may be a thief, from the legs she may become a wanderer. What did God do? He created her from the rib, a modest place, so she may be modest, sitting at home. . . . But even so, women have all these defects."

In Lamentations Rabbah and the international folktale type, the host requests his guest to carve the fowl for the family members gathered around the table. Different parts the guest gives to each one of them reflects the family hierarchy and expresses the honor the guest feels toward the host family. The Midrash Tanhuma, to a large extend misogynistic, describes the idyllic image of women as spouses: modest and concealed at home. It explains that in reality, women are endowed with all the flaws God tried to avoid when he created Eve.

---

2 For an elaborated discussion on this midrash, see Hasan-Rokem 2000.

3 For an elaborated discussion of the tale type see Noy 1965a, 243; 1979, 229.

Our tale creatively combines the two sources:

Fowl Part	Meaning in Lamentations Rabbah and AT International Type	Associated Flaw According to Midrash Tanhuma	Meaning in "Boundaries of Craving"
Wings	Girls leave their father's home	(Hands) A Thief	Fleeing home
Legs	Boys are the home's foundation	Rebelliousness	Vagrancy
Head	The head of the family	Rudeness	Hubris

According to the plot's development, at the end the husband eats the whole chicken by himself and his wife remains hungry. Nevertheless, faithful to her gender role she clears the bowl off the table. The audience is exposed to the abuse of this miserable woman. This abuse raises grievance for the injustice and wrong done to any woman, whoever she is. It is expected that a woman who labored and served savory dishes should herself experience physical gratification from the eating and an emotional one from the diners' reactions. In a Jewish cultural context, this act is considered an offense to the law since according to the *ketubah*—the traditional marriage agreement—the husband is obligated to provide food for his wife.

A plot twist occurs when the wife seeks a way to break this awful routine. She turns to her peer group, who is represented by her female neighbor.[4] The feminine way for solving the issue intends to avoid a direct conflict, and offers instead the use of deceit: eating the chicken but denying doing so. The storyteller is a woman, and it is clear that she identifies herself with the feminine characters of the plot—for example, by adding the title "good" to each one of them: the "good" wife and the "good" neighbor.

---

4 On the intricate role of the neighbor in folk narratives, viewed often as endangering the couple's stability, see Hasan-Rokem 2003, 32–34.

Therefore, it is understandable why the tale neither condemns nor criticizes the lies told to the husband by his wife.

While the wife eats the food she cooked and does not depend on her husband any longer to feed her, the power relation between the two genders changes. Seemingly, her act causes disaster: the death of the infuriated husband. However, the tale does not describe it as a tragic event, but rather turns to humor. The wife is not sad, nor regretful, nor is she lost after losing her spouse, and in the end he is resuscitated. His return to life, though, does not improve the couple's relationship—it is so defective that it cannot be repaired. Only the intervention of an outsider, in this case a judge, brings some sense to the situation. He is the one who decides how they should split the food between them to insure that the couple will be able to continue their shared life.

STONE SOUP

IFA 14701

TOLD BY HEMDA SHAHAM, BULGARIA
RECORDED BY YIFRAH HAVIV

O nce there was a miser who gave almost nothing to his wife. When he left home, he used to leave her only one or two pennies, that's all.

One day, he did not leave her even one penny. His wife did not know what to do. Her neighbors told her: "You have to teach him a lesson so he will wise up."

What did she do? She prepared vegetables and spices and all the best ingredients to make a good soup. She placed the pot on the flame, went out to the yard and took a few smooth stones. She washed them and put them in the pot. When the soup was cooked, she placed it on the stove.

When her husband returned home, he sat at the table and smelled the fragrance of the good soup. He rubbed his hand together and said joyfully: "I smell a nice fragrance. Woman, serve me the soup."

She set the table and served him the steaming soup. The miser swallowed up the soup, drew a spoon or two, and then without paying attention took a stone. Suddenly he screamed: "Hey! What is that?"

"What happened?" asked his wife innocently.

"I almost broke my teeth. What did you put in the soup, woman?" and he took the stone out of his mouth and showed it to her.

She quietly replied: "I made the soup with whatever you left me."

Discussion of
"Stone Soup"

Hemda Shaham, the storyteller, was born in Bulgaria in the early 1940s. Fifty-two of her tales are registered in IFA. They were all recorded by Yifrah Haviv, her brother-in-law. This tale was filed in the archives in 1984.

This tale reflects and structures the distinction between gender roles through food. The conflict at the center of the plot derives from a lack of resources: a miserly husband who does not supply his wife with enough money to purchase foodstuffs and his distressed wife who sees herself committed, according to her gender role, to providing proper food. The wife, unable to solve the conflict by herself, approaches her women neighbors and shares her distress with them.[1] The neighbors, represented in the tale as a collective character, are full participants in their gender role and, like the wife, fulfill it. Their solution to the problem is intriguing. They do not offer to directly cope with the concrete issue, but they propose a devious way to cause her husband to understand the situation.[2] In doing so, they reduce the threat of a damaged marriage, seeking to put it on a better footing. Thus advised, the wife finds a solution by herself.

The soup she prepares is an interesting combination of vegetables and stones. Normally the only mineral used in cooking and common in every kitchen is salt, while the other nutrients come from animals and plants. The wife resorts to adding stones to the dish, showing that the only ingredients

---

1 On the role of women neighbors as a feminine support group, see Hasan-Rokem 2003.

2 This approach is similar to the one described in the previous tale of this chapter, "The Boundaries of Craving."

she has for cooking are from the natural world, and unsuitable for food.[3] According to Lévi-Strauss's models, the more a substance is processed, the more it enters the cultural domain (1969). In the plot, the wife mixes the most obdurate of materials to the food she prepares. She allegedly cooks the stones, but it is an act doomed to failure. Stones, even if cooked for a long time, will not change or undergo a cultural process. In serving the stones, the wife demonstrates her failure, and reflects her situation to her husband, for she has no other alternative but to use ingredients she finds herself.

Note that there is an international tale type called The Soup-Stone whose plot differs from our tale. In this type, the soup-stone needs only the addition of a few vegetables and a bit of meat to make a successful meal (ATU 1548: Uther 2004, 2: 290–91). According to this tale type, a poor person deceives a cook by telling him that he possesses a stone especially for making soup. The poor person asks the cook to give him some more ingredients suitable for making the soup he will prepare using the stone, in order to improve its taste. Both in this tale type and in our tale, use of a stone in cooking is done by a person from a social status lower than the one who is invited to dine. In the tale type, it is the starving poor man who stands in front of the satiated rich one, and in our tale, the wife stands in front of her husband.

Using stones in cooking is in fact an ancient technology: first, stones are heated inside a bonfire and then put in a pot of water. The blazing stones bring the water to a boil (Lévi-Strauss 1997, 33; Kaufman 2006, xxix). The folktales seem to retain the memory of this action and adapt it for a figurative purpose.

---

3 In our day there are food supplements with vitamins and various minerals, but this is not a reality in folktales.

THE BRIDE WHO KNEW IT ALL

IFA 5872

TOLD AND RECORDED BY
MOSHE NEHMAD, PERSIA

O nce my mother's neighbor told her about her daughter-in-law, how she does not listen to her and how she knows everything and does not pay attention in order to learn anything. In fact, the dishes she prepares for her husband, the neighbor's firstborn son, do not succeed at all.

"I don't know," she said, "Why doesn't she want to learn. It annoys me a lot."

"Don't get annoyed," replied my mother, "She eventually will learn in the end. She may be embarrassed to admit to you that she does not know. Now listen and I will tell you about an incident, as I heard it from my mother, may she rest in peace."

My mother used to live in the house of Haj Ibrahim, on the way to the old cemetery, if you remember. His son married the firstborn daughter of Zadok, the rich merchant. Being from a well-established family, she never lifted a finger in cold water while she was living in her father's house. She married and came to live in her in-laws' house. Haj Ibrahim's wife died many years ago and the children grew up in the house of Rachel, their rich aunt.

After the week of banquets, the invited guests, the aunt, and among them the women who cooked, all went back to their homes. The new bride, her name may have been Yocheved, stood with her hands on her head, wondering how she was going to manage her household without the help of Aunt Rachel and the servants. The groom left too, the same day, to attend his father's business. He ordered her to prepare a large and good rice dish for dinner, for he intended to bring back a few guests.

However, this poor girl did not know how to make a fire for the pot. She did not even know how to prepare and how to cook the rice, which she herself liked very much, that it should be ready by evening and suitable for eating. Furthermore, guests were supposed to come and join the meal.

She immediately went to one of her neighbors to ask for her advice. Who would not help a young bride, especially the daughter-in-law of Haj Ibrahim the landlord? Everybody was ready to spend the whole day in her kitchen and cook daily, for their salary would have been ensured. But, the bride refused unequivocally. She might have been afraid that her husband would hear that another woman prepared the meal. Maybe she also wanted to boast her diligence to him. The important thing is that she refused to get any help.

"Just tell me how to do it, and I will cook by myself," said Yocheved to her neighbors, "and I plead to you, please, not to tell anyone. My husband is a strict man."

"So take about four cups of rice," said a neighbor, in despair over the bride's statements, "sort it really well and take out the foreign grains. Beware particularly of small stones."

"I know that" said the bride, "I always helped my mother."

"Then, put a pot full of water on a high flame fire, so it will warm up nicely. Before it boils, take the rice."

"Of course before it boils," the bride interrupted, "I know that."

"Meanwhile, wash the rice really, really well in cold water," continued the neighbor patiently.

"Sure," replied the bride, "I know that. It should be washed twice or three times."

"Then put the rice in the hot water that is on the fire and add salt."

"Well, I know that you are supposed to add salt, a whole spoon," completed Yocheved.

"Cover the pot really well and let the water boil together with the rice."

"Hey, what do you think, that I will remove the rice before the water boils?" replied the bride with a question.

"I see that you are an expert on rice cooking," said the neighbor, maybe in despair, maybe ironically.

"I am not yet an expert," said the bride with excessive humility, "but all you have told me, I know well." Then she turned around and walked away.

"Look, Bride," called the neighbor after her, "once you drain the rice and put it back in the pot, don't forget to add oil in the bottom of the pot, and let it warm up well."

"Ha, oil" said the bride, "you don't have to teach me. This is the most important of all, without the oil the rice won't have any taste."

"If you know everything so well," said the neighbor, biting her lips, "I am sure you won't forget to put a brick of gravel on top of the rice, before covering it with the lid. Don't forget, the most important is the brick!"

"What did you say, a brick?" asked the know-it-all bride, "I will not forget, be sure. I have a gravel brick in the kitchen. This brick will add a lot to the taste and the smell."

She left and went straight to work. She did not forget anything she heard and everything she thought she knew. Not an hour passed and already the rice stood and boiled on the fire and on top of it, proudly cooking, stood the gravel brick as well.

Imagine this, in the evening, the table was set and the expectation was great, both in the groom's heart and the guests' hearts too, waiting to taste the dishes proudly prepared by the hands of the bride. The rice was served; spoons and fingers knocked on the plates and the gravel ground on their teeth. The whole meal was but one big disaster, spitting mud and grinding teeth. On this night, no one tasted any food at all.

"I am certain," my mother concluded, "that it was an excellent lesson for the bride. Because since then she listened carefully to her good neighbor's advice, she closed her mouth, and stopped boasting that she knew it all. Any bride who should start this way, will end up like you and me.

"Ask and ask, you will reach your wanted destination.

"Try to learn a lesson.

"If you are given something, take it."

Discussion of
"The Bride Who Knew It All"

T he storyteller Moshe Nehmad was born in 1918 in Hamadan, at the west of Persia: 34°48′N, 48°31′E. He immigrated to Israel as a young child. He recorded tales from his family members, all of them originating in Persia. Thirty-three of his tales are registered in IFA. This tale was filed in 1964.

This tale is composed of two separate but entwined narratives: a personal one and a humorous anecdote.[1] The personal narrative describes a genuine reality: a woman who tells her friend about the difficulty she encounters with her insubordinate daughter-in-law who refuses to learn from her how to cook.

In traditional Jewish society, cooking skills and knowledge used to be handed down from elderly women to younger ones. In most cases, the mother was the one who prepared her daughter for the task. However, while young brides cooked according to their family's tradition, they had to adapt and learn how to prepare the dishes their husbands were accustomed to. Therefore, the mothers-in-law actually retrained the brides (Bahloul 1983, 189–92).

Hence the woman's distress described in the personal narrative is understandable. As a mother, she is certain that one of her gender roles is to provide food for her family, train her daughter-in-law in cooking, and transmit to her the knowledge required to provide the culinary needs of her son. If she could know that her daughter-in-law were feeding her son satisfactorily, the mother would surely accept her and be ready to see her as her substitute. However, the bride's refusal to learn saddens and disappoints the

---

1 On the phenomenon of folktale entwined with personal tale, see Held 2009.

mother-in-law, who worries her son may not eat properly. In consequence, she has difficulty accepting her as her replacement.

The anecdote embedded inside the personal narrative is presented as an event in a given space familiar to the two women, even though it can be attributed to the general tale type AT 1328*-* (IFA), A Woman Does Not Know Her Housework. At the IFA there are two versions very similar to this anecdote.[2]

Although in the anecdote there is no mention of a mother-in-law, the two narratives together create an intertextual set. The anecdotal plot may provide some relief to the mother-in-law's hardship.[3] The bride in both narratives, the personal one and the anecdote, does not know how to cook and refuses to learn. In the anecdote, the bride is ridiculed and scolded by her husband. Her ignorance and lack of skill is displayed for all to see. This may serve as a symbolic projection to channel the feelings of anger and frustration accumulated by the woman in the personal narrative.

The storyteller is of Persian ethnicity, where rice has a special and important status. It was introduced to Persia over two thousand years ago; there it became a favorite and was combined with other dishes (Marks 2010: 501). Zevulun Kort, of Afghan origin, provides an interesting testimony on the status of rice in Jewish communities of central Asia in a tale he told and recorded, "The Bride Is for Him Who Was Given Good Food" (IFA 1885).[4] Kort comments in his tale: "Afghan Jews used a lot of rice and prepared it

---

2 The two versions deal with a woman who does not know how to cook and seeks the help of a neighbor but does not admit it: "The Smelly Chicken" (IFA 4626), told by Shemuel Rekanati, Sephardic, Israel, recorded by Heda Jason, and "I Know How to Cook but I Like to Ask" (IFA 4593), told by Maurice Eyney, Iraq, recorded by Zvi Moshe Haimovits.

3 The relationship between brides and their mothers-in-law is an intricate one, and is reflected in many folktales. For an extended discussion, see Shenhar 1974, 346–58.

4 Zevulun Kort was a prolific recorder of Afghan tales. At IFA there are over five hundred tales registered in his name. On the close ties between the customs of Persian and Afghan Jews, see Roden 1999a, 389.

in many tasty dishes. The wealthy cooked rice almost daily and each time in a different way . . . when a guest was invited, the main course was rice, served in large plates abundant with rice and meat." Women used to discuss different methods of preparing rice (Shkalim 2006). It served as a sort of testing ground for young brides in assuming their gender role.

In the anecdote, the husband requires his wife to cook rice, and she has to demonstrate her skills not only to him but to the guests he intends to bring home. In despair, she turns to her female neighbors. Curiously, in all three versions of the tale at IFA, the helper is a neighbor and not the mother-in-law. In all three, the neighbors are willing to help the young woman and guide her patiently, but they become infuriated when she refuses to acknowledge the apprenticeship she should undergo.

In our version, anger arises when the bride postures as an experienced person and in so doing refuses her required training. Why is it so irritating? Several answers may be suggested. One is that the unwillingness of the woman to learn is considered a rejection of traditions, norms, and foundations of authority of the society in which she lives. Her refusal can also be interpreted as a rejection of the womanhood hierarchy, according to which the elders are the learned authorities and young women the recipients of their knowledge. Another plausible reason is that apprenticeship is a liminal stage ensuring the bride's proper passage to her new status as a married woman, and her refusal disrupts it. The women close to the bride interpret their role not only to be tutors of cooking skill but also guides helping her to become a complete and capable married wife.

The anecdote describes the various stages in cooking rice. Preparation of the rice prior to its cooking is particularly emphasized—sorting the rice and removing any foreign objects from it, especially stones. This was considered a woman's task. It may also have a broader meaning: according to Jungian symbolism, sorting grains is an expression of the feminine element and its attributes (Neumann 1956; Hartman and Zimberoff 2009). An example is contained in the childhood memoirs of a Persian Jew who helps her grandmother sorting rice: "My grandmother often enticed me to clean the rice with a promise of a story. As she and I inspected piles of rice on a round brass tray, she entertained me with my favorite tale" (Goldin 2003, 91). Indeed, the neighbor in our tale mentions it as one of the preparatory stages: "Sort it really well and take out the foreign grains. Beware particularly of small stones."

The purpose of the sorting is to protect the diners' teeth from being damaged. A woman who insures that the rice is clean of any foreign object demonstrates her concern for her family's welfare and her love for the diners. Symbolically, this act can be interpreted as transitioning food from its natural status to a cultural status, according to the model of Lévi-Strauss.[5] Therefore, when the neighbor tells the bride to put a brick in the rice, as the last stage of the cooking process, this act has an intricate meaning: 1) the bride, who agrees to do it, shows that her training is not completed; 2) her act contradicts the proper cooking process—she removes the food from the culture domain and returns it to the nature domain; and 3) instead of providing for the welfare of her family and the diners, she actually endangers it.

At the end of the anecdote, the situation is rectified. From now on, the bride is ready to listen to her female neighbors and to accept their advice. At this stage, the storyteller returns to the personal narrative (the frame story) and promises that the situation with the "real" bride will improve as well. The bride will join her mother-in-law and her friend and will perform as expected of her.

---

5 See the discussion of the previous tale.

The Second-Rate Challah

IFA 15354

TOLD BY LEAH BLUSHER, LITHUANIA
RECORDED BY CARMELA BLUSHER

I n a small town, a rumor spread: on Shabbat in the rabbi's house, they
ate a "*salene* challah—a second rate challah."[1] The whole town was
frantic.

Hence, the Jewish people turned to the *gabbai*.[2] He claimed that challah baking was a women's issue. Therefore, a committee of three women
was put together with a pious woman who knew all the Shabbat rulings, a
homemaker who knew all about baking, and the third woman, a merchant
from the market. The distinguished delegation arrived at the rabbi's house,
met with his wife and asked her if they indeed ate a *salene* challah at the
rabbi's house on Shabbat. The answer was yes!

The pious woman spoke about Shabbat holiness, which the rabbi's wife
may have not been aware of. The perfect homemaker asked very carefully
if the rabbi's wife knew how to bake a challah, or maybe she did not have
any more fine flour at home because she donated it to charity and that
is why she baked a *salene* challah. Lastly, the merchant did not ask any
question, she just wanted an answer, bottom line, why did they eat a *salene*
challah?

The rabbi's wife answered: Yes, she knows the rules of the Shabbat. No,
she did not give to charity, and the money she gets is enough for house
expenses.

Then the merchant asked her: "So, the bottom line, why?"

---

1 The storyteller explains: this is a challah made of very poor-quality flour. A
good challah is made of the finest wheat.
2 The synagogue manager.

The Rabbi's wife replied: "A rabbi who beats up his wife in the evening so the neighbors won't see, and cuddles with a gentile woman at night so the congregation's leaders won't suspect him, eats a *salene* challah on Shabbat!"

And additionally, that if this is not true and not fair, they should summon her to a Torah trial with Rachel our Matriarch.

Discussion of
"The Second-Rate Challah"

There is no information about the storyteller Leah Blusher, except that two tales are registered in her name at IFA, both recorded by her daughter Carmela Blusher. This one was filed in the archives in 1986.

This tale raises a central issue on the subject of gender and food—food preparation as an expression of the feelings between a couple.

The story deals with a couple's damaged relationship in an ironic way, which enables it to treat such a sensitive and intimate issue in a lighter mode.

The food at the center of the plot is a "second-rate challah," or as the storyteller explains, challah bread made from poor quality flour. The quality of the challah someone eats on Shabbat becomes the concern of all when a public figure is involved, in this case the rabbi of the congregation. In the eyes of society, the quality of the food anyone consumes expresses their social status (Counihan 1999, 8). Furthermore, the quality of the food the rabbi eats reflects his respect for the holiness of the Shabbat. Therefore, the leader of the community should eat the very best quality foods. When it does not occur, the community sees itself obligated to intervene.

The way the community in the tale deals with this matter has a humoristic character to it. The Jews of the town turn first to the *gabbai*—the synagogue's manager—who, according to his function, is closest to the rabbi. The *gabbai* rules that it is a women's matter and so a committee of three women is established. According to Jewish law, women are obligated to observe three mitzvot (commandments) (Mishnah Shabbat 2:6): specific behavior regarding menstruation, lighting candles on Shabbat, and setting aside a part of the dough while baking, which is called, in short, challah. This may be the reason the *gabbai* attributes the whole issue of challah baking to women.

The tale describes with irony the Jewish community and its cumbersome social settings. Each member of this committee oversees a different area: one has knowledge of Jewish law, the second one's expertise is in foodways and food technology, and the third one, a merchant, knows how to evaluate a product's quality. She may also represent straightforward and unrestrained speech.

It is clear that the rabbi's wife is knowledgeable in the two first areas: she knows the Shabbat rulings and she has the means to bake an excellent challah. Still, the question is, why did she prepare an unfit, second-rate challah for the community's rabbi? This question is presented by the merchant. She, a simple woman, asks the main question.

In her answer, the rabbi's wife establishes a correlation between providing food and a couple's tender and loving relationship. According to her view, food has a dimension of honor and status; it is not only a symbol of holiness and Jewish time, but it reflects the couple's intimacy. The rabbi's wife bakes a second-rate challah and in so doing she expresses the lack of respect she feels as a result of her spouse's contemptible behavior. Indeed, the rabbi behaves in a despicable way: he is an abusive, violent, and cheating husband. He fondles a gentile woman while no one can see him. But the ability of the rabbi to perform properly in accordance with the Shabbat ritual requirements depends directly on his wife's Shabbat preparations.

Harmonious relations between spouses are part of the observance of the Torah's commandments concerning relationships between human beings. Therefore, marital cooperation and harmony enables performance of the laws concerning humans and God. In this sense, improper relations between a couple damages a person's relations with heaven.

The rabbi's wife emphasizes at the end of the tale that if the community does not justify her action, she wants Rachel the Matriarch to sentence her. The tale does not provide any explanation of her request, but the connection may be found in the Midrash (Lamentations Rabbah, Petichta 24), where Rachel speaks to God of the tremendous pain she felt when her beloved Ya'acov was with another woman, and how she restrained her sorrow.[1] This behavior granted her privileges when she begged God to be merciful toward the People of Israel. And indeed, she was the only one among the other advocates whose plea was answered.

In our tale, the rabbi's wife, like Rachel the Matriarch, shared her husband with other women, feels betrayed but stays silent, and feels that she has Rachel's support.

---

1 For further study on Rachel in Lamentations Rabbah, see Hasan-Rokem 2000, 126–29.

Woman Raises, Woman Lowers, a Man's Honor Is in a Woman's Hands

IFA 5066

Told by Shlomo Hazan, Morocco
Recorded by Yitshak Wechsler

There was a king and nearby lived a very poor man. Every day the poor man went to the forest, chopped trees, and sold them at the market. With the money he earned, he bought some barley and brought it home. However, his children were so hungry that they could not restrain themselves until their mother prepared them food out of the barley. They used to pounce on the grains and eat them all as is. In the evening, the man used to return home hungry. He cursed his wife and beat her up, for she did not leave food for him.

One time, the king's wife stood by the window and saw how the children grabbed the grains from their mother's hands, not saving a thing for their father. She approached the king and told him: "I have a riddle for you, but don't get angry! Tell me what it is: Woman raises, woman lowers, and man's honor is in a woman's hands."

The king thought she intended to shame him as if, thanks to her, he was king. He got angry with her, took all her beautiful garments from her, put sackcloth on her and banished her from home.

The woman went to the poor man and told him: "I am the queen who lives next to you. At my window, I watch you daily and love entered my heart. I want to marry you."

The poor man saw that the queen spoke wisely and she was pretty, really beautiful, and told her: "Well! I don't mind, if you want, I will marry you."

The man banished his former wife. Just the children stayed with him.

On the first day, he went to work and brought home barley grains. The children wanted to pounce on the grains. What did the queen do? She grabbed a broom and said she will beat up anyone who takes even one grain, and if they do not listen to her, she will kill them. The children were scared to death and did not pounce at all.

The woman cooked the grains, prepared good food, and then called the children. They came, ate and did not even finish it all because the food was very well cooked and cooked food is always more filling and healthy than plain food.

She asked them: "Are you satisfied?"

"Yes," they answered.

The husband came home. She gave him bread from the grains and another dish she prepared. He ate and was satisfied.

On the next day, she put aside some grains and from the rest she baked bread and cooked great food. Everybody was satiated. Every day she secreted away some grains.

One time, when her husband came back from the forest, she told him: "Look, the skin on your back is all bruised. Do not carry wood on your back anymore. Go and buy a donkey."

The husband said: "How should I buy a donkey while I don't have any money?"

She gave him two sacks of barley she stored. He went and bought a donkey. He left again to chop wood and found among them wood from the Kmayre tree.[1] (This wood has a fragrant smell and is very expensive, used also as a cure against disease, and it heals the body. Its fragrance is released especially when burned.)

The woman, who once used to be a queen, recognized immediately the Kmayre and told her husband: "Go and chop a lot of this wood."

He went and brought a lot of it home. She went to the market and sold it piece by piece, and collected a lot of money. Only very rich people bought

---

1 It may refer to the Argan tree, *Argania spinosa*.

this Kmayre wood because it is very expensive. However, it is worth it, for it is very healthy.

At that time, a rich Effendi became impoverished and sold his house in an auction. Many people came, and so too came the woodcutter. Any price that others offered, he gave twice as much. The people got angry with him and wanted to expel him for he was a woodcutter and should not get involved in an auction. The king was there too. He agreed for the wood cutter to participate and threatened him that if he will not pay, he will hang him on the spot. At the end, they all gave up. The woodcutter bought the palace and became as rich as the king, and even more.

When the woodcutter dedicated his new house, his neighbor, the king, came. The woodcutter's wife, the former queen, met him and told him: "Do you remember me? I asked you once to solve a riddle: What is the meaning of woman raises, woman lowers, and man's honor is in a woman's hands? And then you banished me."

The king understood, was ashamed, and was silent.

Discussion of
"Woman Raises, Woman Lowers, a Man's Honor Is in a Woman's Hands"

The storyteller, Shlomo Hazan, was born in 1923 in Imlil, a village situated in the Atlas Mountains of Morocco: 31°7′34″N, 7°55′4″W. He immigrated to Israel in 1952. Twenty-one of his tales are recorded in IFA. This one was filed in 1963.

This tale embodies in a riddle a power struggle between the sexes. The tale praises women's decisive contribution to men's success and household prosperity. The means for this achievement are food preparation and the determination of eating ways. Through these, she influences the financial and social status of her husband and her family.

The tale mentions two women: the woodcutter's first wife and his second wife, the queen. The former fails in fulfilling her gender duties as a mother, wife, and household manager, since her children and husband go hungry. It also seems that love does not prevail between the couple; hence, the husband beats his wife up and easily agrees to replace her with another.

His second wife, the queen, is the complete opposite of his first wife. She seems to represent the ideal of womanhood. Paradoxically, her acts defy the authoritative society's gender order and hierarchy. For even after all her assets as a woman ("her beautiful garments," as the storyteller stated) have been taken from her and she is banished from the palace with only a sackcloth covering her, she succeeds in raising a new family, reestablishing herself, restoring, and even improving upon her previous financial status.

She raises the basic income of her new family and enriches it by maintaining her household in a thrifty and efficient manner.

She operates within her home—an internal and protected space—while her husband does so in public and communal domains—the forest and the market. In these domains, the husband can exchange barley grains hoarded by his wife for a donkey and later cut down valuable wood she has recognized. From its sale he thrives and prospers financially, becoming wealthier than the king himself.

Women's attitudes toward food in this tale are represented in a dichotomous way. The first wife does not cook food and lets her children eat raw, uncooked barley grains.[1] Her nontreatment of the food reflects neglect from which her children and husband suffer. This neglect causes physical and emotional hunger, expressed in the violent response of her husband's beatings, and finally causes her to be expelled from her home and separated from her children. In contrast, the queen is involved in the food's preparation and cooks it thoroughly.

Cooking has various and meaningful aspects. As stated by the storyteller, "The food was very well cooked and cooked food is always more filling and healthy than plain food." Cooking barley is a chemical process causing the breakdown of enzymes that hinder digestion; therefore, it enables more efficient digestion and a feeling of satiety (Baik and Ullrich 2008). Cooking also reflects the effort that a woman invests in her family's well-being; in return, they greet her with appreciation. Cooking is also a process of culturalization, making food available to the family household, turning it into a dish befitting civilized people. In doing so, it changes the family members' behavior from wild to civilized: the children who before used to pounce on the food are now well behaved and the violent husband has turned into a caring one. The tale ends with the answer to the riddle proving the

---

1 About the symbolic meanings of raw food, see Lévi-Strauss 1969; about the very early existence of barley in the human diet, see Marks 2010, 39–40.

correctness of the queen's saying. Thanks to her acts, a woman brings honor to a man, achieving it specifically through food.

It is hard to ignore the way chosen by the queen to keep the hungry children away from the uncooked food: she holds a broom, like a witch, threatening to beat them if they touch the food and to kill anyone who will not listen to her. In a traditional Jewish family, this way of discipline is expected from a man rather than a woman, according to the saying "He that spareth his rod hateth his son: but he that loveth him chasteneth him betimes" (Proverbs 13:24). This is an additional expression of the inversion of gender roles in the tale: the woman breaks traditional boundaries of her gender, becoming the family's central authority figure and, thanks to her, the family prospers. The woman imposes discipline upon her children and proves in the end that the alleged witch, who replaced the biological mother, is the good and giving mother who satisfies their hunger.

The tale belongs to ATU 923B, AT 923B, The Princess Who Was Responsible for Her Own Fortune. At IFA there are over ten different versions of this type.[2]

---

2 See the discussion of one of these versions and a detailed list of the IFA tales belonging to this type: Ben-Amos 2006–11, 3:509–17.

No Answers Are Given
But by Women

IFA 22918

Told by Haji Firji Naji Abu Raya, Muslim, Israel
Recorded by Joram Meron

During the time of the English men, a great quarrel erupted between the Abu Raya family and the El Heleyla clan. The police and the villagers intervened and separated the parties. The police gathered all the men from both sides, Abu Raya and El Heleyla, put them under detention at the Antus family's olive press, and placed guards on them.

The mature and wise women of the Abu Raya family gathered at Saliman Saleh Abu Raya's *madafa* and said: "Tomorrow we have to prepare breakfast for all the detainees at the olive press, and we will do as no one has ever done before."[1]

That night, they quietly started preparing *zalabia* and *feteer meshaltet* and other similar sweets from olden days.[2] They feared that their neighbor, a woman from El Heleyla family, married to the other clan, would hear them and it would get to her family. So they started walking on their toes and pounded the sugar blocks wrapped in fabric strips, so no one should hear.

All the women gathered in silence, and they told them: "Tomorrow, early in the morning, every one of you should dress in her most beautiful garment and adorn herself as if she was going to a wedding."

---

1 The *madafa* is a traditional space for the reception of guests and visitors.
2 *Zalabia* are a kind of sweet fritters; *feteer meshaltet* is a layered pastry originally from Egypt.

In the morning, all the women came dressed and adorned. First walked the elderly women, who were followed by the younger ones and the children. Everyone carried on her head a tray full of all kinds of sweets. They arrived at the olive press and knocked on the door. A police guard saw the women and thought they were going to a wedding. He told them: "You must not, not here, women!"

Ayish El Ibrahim told him: "Open the door for us, and allow my brother Hamad El Ibrahim and El Nadji to see us, and tell them that we have with us breakfast for everybody."

Hamad El Ibrahim and El Nadji opened the door for the women, who started placing the trays in front of the detainees and the police guards. Hamad El Ibrahim and El Nadji stood and respectfully invited first the El Heleyla, the police guards, and the Abu Raya family: "Please partake, the food is ready for all."

After they ate together, they told the police guards: "We reconciled, send us back home."

They asked them: "How can that be?"

They said: "We ate together from one tray and one dish, and that is how we reconciled."

But suddenly, the El Heleyla women arrived, each one on her own, carrying a modest home cooked meal for her husband or her brother.

Their husbands told them: "Go back! The wise women from the Abu Raya family prepared for us a banquet and reconciled between us. And now we are returning home."

Discussion of

"No Answers Are Given But by Women"

The storyteller, Haji Firji Naji Abu Raya, was born in 1939 in the city of Sakhnin in northern Israel: 32°52′N, 35°18′E. Her tale was recorded as a part of the late Joram Meiron's project to record tales from Arab villages in the Galilee (Meron 2005–12). This tale was filed in the archives in 2004.

The tale refers to historical events, people, families, and sites during a period called in the tale "the time of the English men," which corresponds to the British Mandate period in Palestine (1918–48).

The tale presents differences between the genders and clearly favors the female. It starts by exposing a feud between the men of two clans living in Sakhnin: Abu Raya and El Heleyla. The people trying to separate the quarrelers are also men: the police and the townsmen. The men's strategy to deal with the conflict is separation, distancing themselves from home and confinement. However, it does not solve the fundamental problem, which is the disagreement between the two sides.

In contrast, the clans' women seek to restore comradeship and peace between the rivals. They do so by using the woman's strategy of preparing food for all the men. They take upon themselves the role of a sort of universal mother who feeds her children. The women's attempt to end the men's conflict is a subversive act, as it contains criticism of the men's conduct. Within the cultural context, the method they employ is subversive too: in Arab society, a shared meal seals a *sulha*—the peacemaking ritual between rivals.[1] In

---

1 About the *sulha* ritual see Lang 2002.

this tale, the women initiate a shared meal and by doing so they are the ones who create the *sulha*.

The women choose to prepare delectable, festive dishes reserved for special public events such as weddings. Sharing food in public has the purpose, among others, to create bonds and formal alliances (Weiss 2010, 24). It is a sign of kinship, trust, and friendship (Counihan 1999, 12–13). Some even see commensality and sharing food as what defines us as humans (Loichot 2018, 170)

The women's strategy leads to the desired result. The men receiving the dishes follow their hosting code—they invite first their opponents to join the meal and they include the guards as well. The shared festive meal produces peace; as the men say in the tale, "We ate together from one tray and one dish, and that is how we reconciled."

Even though the concluding scene of the tale seems idyllic, the rivalry between the clans is so deep that it is present throughout the whole plot up to its end. Contrary to expectation, the women who initiated the meal, belonging to one clan, do not include in their preparations the women of the other clan. They gather secretively in the house of one of their own, cook bountiful delicacies, and serve them to all the men. Their performance is the opposite of the other clan's women who, each one separately, brings a modest dish for their husband's or brother's breakfast.

Despite the title, "No Answers Are Given but by Women," the answer is not given by all women but solely by the Abu Raya clan, characterized in the tale as "the wise." The storyteller, who belongs to the Abu Raya clan, shows admiration for women, but specifically for the women of her own clan.

3

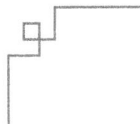

WITH A GOOD EYE
AND FROM ALL
THEIR HEARTS

FOOD AND CLASS

F ood plays an important role in social systems and is entwined in their interactions: type and quality of food point to a person's economic and social status (Counihan 1999, 8; Goode 1992). Sharing food and eating together—*commensality*—tie and reinforce social bonding, defining members of families, social groups, and religions (Loichot 2018, 170). Hosting is a way to create new alliances (Selwyn 2000, 19). Consuming a meal together has a purpose—among others, to draw its participants closer to each other (Kraemer 2007, 28; Weiss 2010, 24). In extreme cases, it can also save a person's life: "In its extreme outcomes, commensality exists alongside the possibility that people starve if not included in shared meals" (Julier 2013, 4). On the other side, not sharing food can result in violence and mutiny (Archer 2014, 5–15).

In Jewish culture, in addition to these functions, food is also a means to establish mutual social responsibility. A person is obligated to provide food for the needy as part of the Torah's interpersonal ethical directives. Strictly observing these is just a part of the broader context of the relations between humans and God. For example, ancient farmers had the duty to leave some of the crops for the needy (Segal 2014, 1697). This duty is described in several biblical laws:

> And when ye reap the harvest of your land, thou shalt not wholly reap the corners of thy field, neither shalt thou gather the gleanings of thy harvest: And thou shalt not glean thy vineyard, neither shalt thou gather every grape of thy vineyard; thou shalt leave them for the poor and stranger. (Leviticus 19: 9–10)

> At the end of three years thou shalt bring forth all the tithe of thine increase the same year, and shalt lay it up within thy gates: And the Levite (because he hath no part nor inheritance with thee), and the stranger, and the fatherless, and the widow, which are within thy gates, shall come, and shall eat and be satisfied; that the Lord thy God may bless thee in all the work of thine hand which thou doest. (Deuteronomy 14: 28–29)

> When thou cuttest down thine harvest in thy field, and hast forgot a sheaf in the field, thou shalt not go again to fetch it: it shall be for the stranger, for the fatherless, and for the widow: that the Lord thy God may bless thee in all the work of thine hands: When thou beatest thine olive tree, thou shalt not go over the boughs again: it shall be for the stranger, for the fatherless, and for the widow: When thou gatherest the grapes of thy vineyard, thou shalt not glean it afterward: it shall be for the stranger, for the fatherless, and for the widow. (Deuteronomy 24: 19–22)

> When thou hast made an end of tithing all the tithes of thine increase the third year, which is the year of tithing, and hast given it unto the Levite, the stranger, the fatherless, and the widow, that they may eat within thy gates, and be filled. (Deuteronomy 26: 12)

This duty is presented as a divine, holy decree that should be respected: "Thou shalt leave them for the poor and stranger: *I am the Lord your God*" (Leviticus 19: 10).

Added to the religious requirement is an ethical human aspect: the people of Israel should remember their origin as a group of poor slaves, dependent on others' benevolence for their physical existence: "And thou shalt remember that thou wast a bondman in the land of Egypt, therefore I command thee to do this thing" (Deuteronomy 24: 22). This memory is the foundation for the empathy a Jewish person should feel toward the bitter fate of people and the suffering of any needy person met on their way.

The ethical aspect of relating to the other as a reflection of the self, expressed through food representations, is present also in the writings of the prophets. For example: "Is it not to deal thy bread to the hungry, and that thou bring the poor that are cast out to thy house? When thou seest the naked, that thou cover him; and that thou hide not thyself from thine own flesh?" (Isaiah 58:7).

Over the centuries, Jewish culture established permanent institutions such as charity funds and food collections in order to provide for the needy (Gardner 2015). Medieval Jewish philosopher Maimonides describes the process in detail:

> Every town where Jews reside has to appoint charity managers, people well known and trustworthy. They should go door to door from Shabbat's eve to Shabbat's eve, and take from everyone the proper and allotted amount. And they should distribute the allowances from Shabbat's eve to Shabbat's eve, and provide each poor with food sufficient for seven days. This is called the charity fund. Thus, managers should be appointed to collect daily from every yard bread and other food and fruits or money from the willing at the time. Every evening they should distribute their collection to the poor, and give each one a daily livelihood. This is called

tamhui [the food pool]. (*Mishneh Torah*, Zeraim, laws of gifts to the poor, 1: 1–2)

All, including the poor themselves, were obligated to contribute, even if their contribution was meager. For example: "A poor person who gave a cent to the charity box and a slice of bread to the soup kitchen, those are received. If he does not give anything, he is not required to give" (Toseftah Peah [Lieberman] 4:10).

In addition to these, various Jewish communities developed local customs such as hosting poor people for the Shabbat meal. This custom was described in a folktale: "According to the holy custom in the Jewish towns, the beggars gathered on Shabbat's eve by the synagogue portal and the rich and honorable as they exited the shul, were taking one of them home, for the Shabbat's meal" (IFA 2000), "Guest on Shabbat's Eve."

Folktales focusing on food and class do not represent merely the social solidarity that tradition was seeking to establish. They expose intricate social stratums, psychological realities, and difficulties inherent in giving and receiving help, even to the point of subversion. They examine the dissonance existing between the society's expectations and individuals' willingness or unwillingness to behave accordingly. Folktales do not consider just the aid givers but also those who receive it and their real needs.[1] This issue is also discussed in Jewish law. For example, "One who has food for two meals should not take food from the *tamhui*, and one who has food for fourteen meals should not take from charity funds" (Mishnah Pehah 8:7).

The folktales also warn against the parasitic attitude that may develop in a society in response to its obligation to help the needy. The complex emotional aspects of getting help are investigated as well. In numerous tales, the conflict leading the plot is between a hungry person begging for

---

1 See also Maimonides (Mishnei Torah, Zeraim, laws of gifts to the poor, chapters 9, 10), Shulhan Arukh Yorei Dea, laws of Charity 253, 1.

food and a rich miser who, apathetic to his distress, is unwilling to share his table's delicacies with the needy.

Seven tales are included in this chapter. Two focus on the universal conflict between the hungry and the satiated. Five additional tales focus on Jewish society's particular values and examine their implementations.

Christian Hell and Jewish Hell

IFA 3346

Told by Berl Rabinovitch, Belarus
Recorded by Zalman Baharav

Once there was a man who was very involved with people, always seeking out justice and honesty in this world, but found it all to be lies.

One night this man dreamt he goes to heaven. There, he walks through its different sections. The angel who is in charge of these places and who takes care of the guests shows him the dwelling place of the righteous—heaven. There the righteous of the world sit with crowns on their heads and enjoy the Divine Presence's radiance.

The wicked are found on the lower floor and receive their due punishment. The man wanted to see hell. The angel introduced him to a large hall, close to a table prepared with all the bounty of the earth. All kinds of food and drinks—roasted pigeons, stuffed ducks, diverse delicacies usually offered to kings and counts—are piled high on this table. Around the table, many people are seated. On each one's neck hangs a cross. But each one of them is thin and gaunt. They do not taste the dishes and look very sad. This fellow understood that they were Christians, confined to this hell prepared especially for them. He asked them: "In front of you is a dressed table, all the delicacies of the world are here and you are hungry? Your faces show that you do not taste the food placed here in abundance."

They replied to him: "This is our punishment. Each one of us received a fork a meter and a half long. Our arms are short and it is impossible to bring the food to our mouths. This is why we do not eat at all."

The man told them: "Stupid people, Ivan should bring his fork with the delicious dishes to the mouth of Nikita, George should feed Franz,

Stefan should stuff Mikael, and Fritz should feed Keler, and so on with all the others."

They accepted the advice and in doing so were saved from hell's punishment.

A short time later, the same person entered the Jewish hell. He recognized them. Their noses were a witness that they were Abraham's descendants. This company also sits around a table covered with succulent dishes: boiled meat, turkeys roasted in fat, omelets of all sorts of eggs on a frying pan. And here too, their faces show that a horrid emptiness prevails in their belly. A great sadness is visible in their eyes. He told them: "You too have long forks, and this is why you do not eat?" They answered him: "Yes, this is the reason." He told them: "Avraham, Isaac, Ezekiel, and Amnon should take their forks, stick them in the chunks of meat in front of them and feed Moshe, Menahem, Jacob, and Baruch. You will all be satiated and deride the sentence."

Avraham, Isaac, Ezekiel, and Amnon opened their mouths and said: "What do you mean? Why? We are not giving them a thing even if they will explode here. Indeed they are our brothers, that is why they should take their food by themselves."

Discussion of
"Christian Hell and Jewish Hell"

T he storyteller, Berl Rabinovitch, was born in 1870 in Parichi
        in the Bobruisk district in eastern Belarus: 52°48″N, 29°25″E.
        His son Zalman Baharav recorded his tales, four of which are
registered at IFA. This one was filed in the archives in 1960.

This tale resolutely criticizes, although with a grin, the arbitrariness existing within Jewish society. This maliciousness appears through the unwillingness of the Jews sentenced to hell to assist one another, refusing, at the
price of suffering self-starvation, to feed their fellow men even though it
requires minimum effort on their part.

This criticism is not expressed openly, but is channeled through two
means of distancing: one is the plot taking place in a dream and the second
one is that in the dream the environment described is supernatural, remote
from human reality—heaven and hell. However, it seems obvious that the
description of hell has a plausible human reality.

In IFA's collection, there are three versions of this tale, all of them from
Eastern Europe.[1] Another close relative is included in Alter Druyanov's
Book of Jokes and Witticisms:

> Rabbi Haim of Romshishok sermoned in public and told: Once I went
> up to heaven and entered hell. I looked and saw: old and young people
> sit in rows in front of tables covered in abundance, and on each one's arm

---

1 "The Long Spoons" (IFA 1514); "Better Die Than Help" (IFA 9776);
    "Moishele's Hell" (IFA 7670).

a long spoon is attached and they cannot reach their own mouth because of the length. And so they all sat, in rows facing each other in despair while great sadness showed on their faces. I approached one of them and told him: "Fool! Your eyes see all this plenty and crave, take your spoon and feed your fellow man seated in front of you and he in return will feed you with the spoon tied to his arm." The man looked at me angrily and replied: "I prefer to look and crave all day long rather than see him enjoy and sated for an hour." I was shocked, a great cry came out of my mouth, and I woke up. (Druyanov 1963, tale #1884)

The complete plot does not fit one tale type exactly, but the part about feeding with long spoons may refer the tale to the international types The Long Spoons (ATU 821 B*)[2] and Devil as Host at Dinner (AT 821 B*).

The tale's narrator, particularly in his description of heaven, combines elements from the Jewish tradition together with universal folk elements. At the beginning of the story, the narrator introduces a man who found this world "all to be lies," intending maybe that humans in general are liars. This notion is present in a midrash about an argument raised in heaven preceding the creation of Adam:

R. Simon said: When the Holy One, blessed be He, came to create Adam, the ministering angels formed themselves into groups and parties, some of them saying: "Let him be created" while others urged: "Let him not be created." Thus, it is written: "Mercy and truth are met together; righteousness and peace have kissed each other" (Psalms 85:10). Love said: "Let him be created, because he will dispense acts of love." Truth said: "Let him not be created, because he is compounded of falsehood." (Bereshit Rabbah 8:5)

---

2 In IFA are three additional versions of this tale type but their plot does not include descriptions of heaven: IFA 31 from Turkey; IFA 3623 from Iraqi Kurdistan; IFA 7126 from Hungary.

An additional element from Jewish tradition is the description of the fate of the righteous in Paradise, who receive spiritual reward: their heads are decorated with crowns and they enjoy the sight of divination: "In the future world there is no eating, nor drinking, nor propagation, nor business, nor jealousy, nor hatred, nor competition, but the righteous sit with their crowns on their heads feasting on the brightness of the divine presence" (Babylonian Talmud, Berachot 17a).[3]

In the tale, there is reference to heaven's different sections and the angel who guides humans through them. These descriptions can be found in Jewish traditional sources, although not often. For example: "These sections are the upper section and the lower section and air and four upper ones" (Avot DeRabbi Natan 37:7). So too: "Each group has its own section in Paradise, and opposed to them there are seven groups in hell" (Yalkut Shimoni, Psalms 656). A guiding angel is mentioned as well: "When an Israelite dies, there is an angel in charge in Paradise who takes every circumcised son of Israel and brings him to Paradise" (Midrash Tanhuma 96:14). And ascents to heaven and angels' guided tours through its premises are described in detail in Apocrypha and Pseudepigrapha texts such as the Ascension of Isaiah, the Apocalypse of Baruch, and the Book of Enoch.

However, the description of the set tables covered in abundance in hell, although present in many folktales around the world,[4] are lacking in Jewish traditional sources. Our tale, as well as the three additional versions in IFA, adopts the narrative framework of the international type but bears an essential variation. In the international type, the core issue is the difference between an almost identical Paradise and hell. In both places, tables are plentifully stocked with food and in both people have long spoons, or long

---

3 In Jewish sources, there is another view as well. According to it, in the world to come, the righteous will participate in a banquet (see chapter 1 in the present book).

4 For example the tale's Chinese version, called "Heaven and Hell" (Chang 1969: 47–49).

sticks in the versions from Asia. For example, a Japanese version of the tale, mentioned by Mitsugi Saotome:

> I am reminded of an old Japanese folktale of an adventurous young man who wanted to know the difference between heaven and hell. He first looked upon hell and saw many people seated at a long table filled with the finest foods. But everyone had gaunt faces with sunken cheeks. They were thin and weak, crying in despair. A closer look revealed that their hands had only two fingers formed into the shape of hashi, Japanese chopsticks, four feet long. Although they could pick up the food, their fingers were so long that they could not get it into their mouths. In frustration they were turning their tools into weapons, fighting selfishly among themselves for the food they could not eat. Then he looked upon heaven. He saw the same long table with the same beautifully prepared food and the same long fingers. But everyone was laughing and smiling at the others. Their cheeks were full and glowing with health. There was no fighting, for they picked up the food and, extending it to the other side of the table, fed each other. What is the difference between heaven and hell? Consciousness, compassion, and cooperation. (Saotome 2013, 127)

In these tales, the only difference between Paradise and hell is that in Paradise people are feeding each other, and therefore they are satiated and happy, while in hell they refuse to do so and stay hungry, gaunt, and angry. The message is clear: selfishness, egotism, and the unwillingness to assist the "other" create hell, even among living people. Interestingly, it is a message that aligns with the perspective of the existentialist philosopher Jean-Paul Sartre, who in his play *No Exit* describes hell as composed of appalling human relationships (Sartre 1947).

As stated, the Jewish versions differ from the international plot. Paradise is described according to a Jewish point of view, where food is not an essential part: the righteous are crowned and admire the Divinity's radiance, according to the description of the adorned Righteous in the midrash Bereshit Rabbah (8:5). The comparison is not between Paradise and hell but rather between two hells, the Christian one and the Jewish one. There is but one difference between them and it is the food served in each.[5] It is interesting to notice that the gentile food is not represented by meat dishes forbidden according to the Jewish dietary laws. It includes roasted squabs and fattened ducks, permitted for consumption by Jews, if slaughtered properly, but this point is not raised in the plot. The food served in the Jewish hell does not differ essentially from the one served in the Christian one. It includes meat, boiled, says the narrative, instead of roasted, while both ways are permitted. Other dishes, which were a part of Jewish cuisine as well, are mentioned: turkey meat in fat and omelets. It is possible that fat is a sign of kosher Jewish cuisine, while Christians could use butter in the cooking of fowl.[6]

In the Jewish versions of the tale, the Christians are ready to feed each other, and in doing so they end their suffering. As opposed to them, the Jews refuse to help one another and prefer to suffer hell's torments. Criticism of Jewish society, its wickedness and miserliness, is bitter and the message is a clear one: the social reality in which Jews fail to assist one another is hell on earth.

Nevertheless, this tale retains an optimistic overtone: whenever the Jews should become willing to help one another, a very easy act to perform, their suffering due to poverty and hunger will come to an end and their condition will improve.

5 See the next chapter on the role of food in reinforcing social identity.
6 See for example a Polish recipe for a roasted turkey cooked in milk butter: "Winner Winner, Turkey Dinner—Polish Style," Polish Classic Cooking, accessed December 27, 2020, http://www.polishclassiccooking.com/2011/11/winner-winner-turkey-dinner-polish.html.

Hosts Who Do Not Feed Their Guest

IFA 2400

Told by Shemuel Rekanati, Sephardic, Israel
Recorded by Rachel Seri

Fifty years ago, a rabbi from *Eretz Israel* was sent on a mission to the Jewish communities of Turkey, to the town of Çanakkale. The rabbi of Çanakkale came to meet the rabbi from *Eretz Israel*, received him with great honor, brought him home, and offered him refreshments, food, and drinks.

Back then, fifty years ago, they were guests, or more precisely, the hosts used to receive guests generously, with a good eye and with all their hearts. They treated guests with a lot of respect; so much so that they all ate together from the same delicious, steaming, and fragrant dish.

The hosting rabbi recited the blessing *Netilat Yadayim* (the hand washing blessing) and *ha-Motzi* (the blessing over the bread) and immediately he dipped his piece of bread in the dish, not removing it to put it in his mouth. He waited for his wife to dip her piece of bread. Then his wife dipped her piece of bread and did not lift it up from the dish until her husband was ready to dip bread again. And so the host and the hostess kept the dish just for themselves and gobbled down the whole dish. The guest, the rabbi from *Eretz Israel*, wondered about what he just saw and on his hosts' behavior. He did not have the audacity to compete with them in pushing and dipping his bread, which stayed in his hand and failed to even have a first dip. He stayed hungry, his belly empty, and he did not manage to taste the food offered to him.

His hosts finished the whole dish. And after the plate was empty, the host told his guest: "Very well, stay with us, be our guest a few more days." He pleaded with him to remain with them and not be hosted by others.

The next day, the guest learned his hosts' wisdom and decided to behave like them, his stomach empty with an irritating hunger. At the mealtime, the hostess brought a steaming, fragrant, delicious, and appetizing dish. Even before the host was able to finish the blessing over the bread, the guest immediately dipped his bread and did not lift it until the hostess dipped hers. He hinted to the hostess to not lift her bread until his piece was ready for another dip, and the woman obeyed him. The guest from *Eretz Israel* and the hostess ate in haste the steaming food and did not let the host dip his bread and he stayed hungry.

After they finished and emptied the plate, the host told the guest: "Dear guest sent from *Eretz Israel*, you can return to Israel, for you have accomplished your mission. This is not worth it for me. You can go and end your stay with me."

Discussion of
"Hosts Who Do Not Feed Their Guest"

T he storyteller, Shemuel Rekanati, was born in 1897 in the Old City of Jerusalem. He heard many folktales in his childhood from his mother and elderly neighbors in the Old City. In IFA, 362 tales are registered in his name. This tale was filed in the archives in 1960.

This tale deals with the dissonance between the Jewish culture's moral values of hosting generously and providing physical and financial support to *Eretz Israel*'s emissaries and the miserly and resentful people who do not abide by them. These difficult issues are approached with humor, allowing for an easier acceptance of them.

The tale is an anecdote, which is, by definition, "a short humorous story that reports on a real event and is connected to people who live in reality and are usually mentioned by their full name" (Alexander 1999, 381). This tale can be ascribed to the international tale type ATU 1568*, The Master and the Farmhand at the Table. Uther's characterization of this type fits the plot of our story: "A farmer and his farmhands help themselves to food out of a common dish. The farmwife always places the dish so that the best piece of meat lies near the farmer" (Uther 2004, vol. 2, 309).

In our tale, the plot occurs in a specific time and place and the characters are identified according to their functions. The storyteller tells the story as an event that took place over fifty years ago in the Turkish town of Çanakkale, a port city in northwestern Anatolia: 40°09′21″N, 26°24′49″E. The Jewish community that lived there mostly comprised descendants of Spanish Jews.

This tale was sent to IFA in 1960, therefore the plot's timeframe is the beginning of the twentieth century. The main characters are the city's rabbi and his wife as well as an emissary from *Eretz Israel*.[1] At that time, hosting emissaries from *Eretz Israel* in Turkey was common. For example, during the years 1870–1908, eight emissaries visited Turkey on nine different occasions, four of whom visited Anatolia: Rabbi Shlomo Moshe Suzin in 1892, Rabbi Yaakov Danon in 1893 and 1895, Rabbi Avraham Bejajo in 1907, and Rabbi Aharon Ferera in 1908 (Gaon 1928, 289). Therefore, even if the story is not an accurate record of a particular occurrence, it is certainly based on documented events.

The story is composed of three parts. In the first part, the action takes place in public, in front of the community. The rabbi walks toward the emissary from *Eretz Israel*, receives him with all due respect, brings him home, and offers him refreshments. In doing so, he behaves according to the society's values. In summarizing this part, the narrator emphasizes the desired rules of conduct with regard to receiving guests properly: "With a good eye and all his heart." The honor granted to the guest is expressed in the fact that he is invited to share a delicious, hot meal from a common plate, emphasizing the connection between the diners.

In the second part of the story, the action takes place in the rabbi's home, in a private space far from the community's sight. At first, it seems that the hosts continue to behave according to the desired etiquette and accepted norms. The rabbi follows the rules of Jewish ritual. At the beginning of the meal, he washes his hands, recites the blessing accordingly, and blesses the bread. This refers to the blessing that opens the meal according to Mishnah Berachot 6:1: "How does one bless the fruits? . . . On the bread he says: 'He who brings forth bread from the land'." Immediately afterward, he is the first to dip his piece of bread into the dish served in a common plate. His wife follows him. This is where the dissonance begins. One can reasonably assume that the proper way to honor a guest is to let him be the first to partake of the food. Since in our tale the host eats first, this can be

---

1 For the history of emissaries of the "Old Yishuv" from *Eretz Israel* to Jewish communities in the Diaspora, see Yaari 2002.

explained by the host's desire to show his guest the way they eat together. Later, however, the situation becomes clear. The couple waits for each other before they take the bread out of the plate and do not allow their guests to eat, so that he remains hungry. Ironically, he is then invited by his host to stay longer at their house.

In the third part of the story, the plot takes a twist and the situation is reversed. The guest mimics the behavior of his host and shares the dish with the host's wife. The paired eating now shared by the guest and his host's wife takes on a dimension of intimacy,[2] like stealing the spouse. The guest takes over not only the host's food but also his wife. This time the host is left physically and emotionally hungry following abandonment by his wife. He is punished for having so blatantly violated the mitzvah of hospitality and thus allowing his wife to do so. The frustrated rabbi informs the guest that this is the end of the mission. This is not a "corrective" turn; the audience is not told if the rabbi has changed his ways. We can assume probably not.

The story expresses a more general, implicit criticism of Jewish society abroad. This society declares that it supports the Jewish settlement in the Land of Israel, but in fact it cares first for its own welfare, leaving the settlers "hungry," without resources and supporters.

---

2 On the close connection between eating and intimacy, see chapter 2.

THREE GREAT MITZVOT

IFA 11180

TOLD AND RECORDED BY
AVRAHAM KEREN, POLAND

Once on a summer day, a Jewish beggar brought home a guest. His wife tells him: "What did you do? What will I offer him?"

Her husband answered her: "Oh well, we will eat a few spoons less, so there will be food for the guest. What did you prepare?"

"Borscht."

"And what else?"

"A few potatoes."

"Hey, this is good, real king's food."

All of a sudden, the wife remembered and said: "I have some leftover fish I saved from Shabbat and I put it on the windowsill, it is cool there. Who shall I give this piece of fish to?"

Her husband replied: "Give it to the guest."

And so the wife did. The guest ate the fish, thanked them, and went home.

A few days later, the Jewish beggar tells his wife that the poor man got a stomach sickness and he suffers from diarrhea. The wife went to visit him. After some time, the beggar comes home and tells his wife: "You know, our poor guest, he died."

Sure enough, the wife went to the funeral.

After her return, she told her husband with great satisfaction: "Thank God! With the leftover fish I was able to perform three mitzvot: hospitality, visiting the sick, and accompanying the deceased."

Discussion of
"Three Great Mitzvot"

Avraham Keren, the storyteller, was born in 1912 in Bircza, a village in southeast Poland, situated at 49°41′32″N, 22°28′46″E. A Holocaust survivor, he immigrated to Israel in 1948. In IFA, ninety tales are registered that he himself recorded as he remembered hearing them from his parents and siblings, and 347 additional tales of his were recorded by various storytellers. This tale was filed in the archives in 1976.

This is a short anecdote that brings to an absurdity the mitzvah, a religious good deed, of hospitality and the desire to observe mitzvot in general. The story tells of a Jewish beggar and his wife who wish to observe the mitzvah of hospitality. They host a poor person like themselves and share with him their meager food, an act with tragic consequences: their guest dies of food poisoning caused by eating a piece of fish that the two had served him, not realizing it was spoiled.

The meager economic situation of the couple is represented in the story by the food they consume. The dishes mentioned—borscht[1] and potatoes—are a symbol of their low socioeconomic status.[2] This is the food that shows up on the tables of the poor, but this couple considered them to be "royal dishes." Although these dishes are presented as food for the poor,

---

1 On the soup called borscht, or *hamitzah* in Hebrew, its history and sources, see Marks 2010, 64–66.
2 According to Barthes's terms; see Barthes 1961.

they characterize the Jews of Eastern Europe in general,[3] and they remained part of their diet even when the economic situation of the Jews improved after their immigration to the West.[4]

Despite the poverty, illness, and death described in the tale, this is a humorous story. The comic elements are based on the principle of *appropriate incongruity*, "an appropriate relationship between categories that would ordinarily be regarded as incongruous" (Oring 1992, 1–15; Oring 2003, 1). The discrepancy appears twice in two different parts of the plot. The first discrepancy is related to the piece of fish that the hosts serve their guest and the understanding that the fish is spoiled. At the beginning of the story, the listeners hear that it was a summer day and then that the fish had been lying outside for a few days: "I have some leftover fish I saved from Shabbat and I put it on the windowsill, it is cool there." Hence, the listeners can already understand at this point that the fish is spoiled. This is beyond the woman's grasp, who innocently thinks that the windowsill is a cool place. The comic element in the story is created by the lack of correspondence between what the listeners understand and what the woman and her husband understand, or rather what they do not understand. The comical element is also due to the gap between the couple's good intentions and their unfortunate consequences.

The second discrepancy appears at the end of the story. The couple, who caused the death of their guest, do not feel any responsibility or any guilt and are satisfied that they have fulfilled three commandments. Their obliviousness of the consequences of their actions, and simultaneously their sense of self-satisfaction, create the comic effect.

---

3 On the centrality of the potato in the food of the Jews of Eastern Europe, see Marks 2010, 483; Roden 1999b, 131.

4 See, for example, J. Friedlander 1986; Jochnowitz 2011.

The audience feels sympathy toward the couple for several reasons: they accept their fate without any protest, they are satisfied with the little they share, they show generosity toward the other poor person, and they offer him food even at the cost of reducing their portions. In their eyes, they served him the best dish. Therefore, the story does not arouse laughter at all, but a sad smile at their naïveté, their kindness, and the poor Jew's fate.

This story is not common. This is the only version recorded at IFA.[5]

---

5 Among the 180 jokes about the poor in the Druyanov collection (1963), only two jokes (# 296, 297) deal with the matter of inviting a beggar to a poor person's house. As in the tale discussed here, at first the host's wife is not enthusiastic, to say the least. Besides this, their plots are completely different from the one before us: 296—"A poor man invited a beggar to dinner, and when they entered, the poor man's wife said poetically: 'The Dead and the Deceased provide for each other' "; 297—"A poor man brought back from the synagogue two beggars to host for a meal. . . . His wife was angry: The pauper invites guests to an empty cauldron."

A Guest for Shabbat

IFA 13385

Told by Mordechai Hillel Kroshnitz, Poland
Recorded by Ayelet Etinger

In a small town lived a rich Jew, a property owner, but he was a big miser too.

One Friday after the Shabbat prayers, he decided to be generous and to host one of the poor persons who came to town, waiting at the synagogue to be invited by Jewish families. The rich man returned home with his guest. After *Netilat Yadayim* (the ritual hand washing) and the *Kiddush*—(the blessing over wine), they all sat down to eat the Shabbat dinner.

The poor guest, who was starving, ate all the food served at the table: fish, chopped liver, beef stock, *tzimess*—(sweet carrots), together with challah bread. He ate everything with challah, although on the table there was also sliced daily bread.

The rich man noticed that and got furious, for challah is much more expensive than daily bread and even he and his family ate the liver and the meat with regular bread. Finally, he lost his patience. He turned toward the guest and asked him: "Why, my guest, do you eat everything with challah?"

The guest replied: "I am used to eating everything, even soup, with challah or bread."

"So why do you eat only challah and do not even taste the regular bread?" asked the host.

"Because the challah is so much tastier, especially the sweet challah with raisins," replied the guest.

"But it is more expensive," said the rich host.

"I figured that, but it's worth it," answered the guest calmly and continued feasting.

Discussion of
"A Guest for Shabbat"

This tale was told by Mordechai Hillel Kroshnitz, describing a situation in the life of an extinct Jewish community in Eastern Europe.[1] This tale was filed in the archives in 1981. Three other versions of the story from Poland are recorded in IFA.[2]

Contrary to what might be expected, the tale is not nostalgic about the past but critically examines the social gaps that existed in the society at the time. On the one hand, Jewish society sought to bridge its economic gaps by hosting poor people at a Shabbat meal in wealthy homes. On the other hand, it had not succeeded in changing the character of the two economic extremes in the society: the miserly rich man who hosts poor people in his home for the wrong reasons and the poor soul who exploits the hospitality and eats the precious challah.

The Shabbat meal described in the tale is taken from reality. The dishes mentioned are part of the Shabbat meal of Ashkenazic Jewry today.[3] Gaps between the rich and the poor are demonstrated through a social signifier: the type of bread eaten. The challah, which is the most precious and finest of breads, is eaten every Shabbat, in the sacred time, and its nature can vary. The challah of the rich man in this tale is a challah with raisins,

---

1 For information on this storyteller, see discussion of tale IFA 14221 in chapter 1.

2 The other versions are: "Challah Cost a Lot" (IFA 8177), told by Malka Gutter, Poland, and recorded by her daughter Aliza Shenhar; "I Did Not Come Here to Enjoy" (IFA 2795), told by Segal Yakov Goldberg, Poland, and recorded by David Ofir; and "The Wise Visitor" (IFA 4802), told by Yosef Cedar, Poland, and recorded by his son Fishel Cedar.

3 On Shabbat meal in Eastern Europe, see Roden 1999a: 52.

which is considered the most precious and tasty form of challah. At the other extreme, black bread is the cheapest type of bread and is eaten on weekdays.[4]

The plot unfolds across two spaces. One is the public space of the synagogue, where the rich man wishes to show his generosity and invites the poor man to his home for the Shabbat eve meal. The other space is the private space, the house of the rich man. In the private space, far from the eyes of the audience, the two characters, rich and poor, deviate from the accepted norms of hospitality. At first, it seems that the rich man behaves in the manner expected of him. He performs the rituals related to eating, washing his hands and making a blessing over wine, and then he shares the copious meal with the poor man. The ideal hospitality, which does not exist here, is to be generous and to respect the guest without conditions. The rich man does not succeed in being guided by a genuine sense of giving. His stinginess overcomes him and he disrespects his guest. At the same time, the poor man also deviates from the rules of hospitality. We expect him to act with restraint, imitate the behavior of the other diners, and eat according to what is customary in the host's home. However, he takes full advantage of the circumstances, eats everything, and chooses to eat only the finest challah while the others eat the cheaper bread. The dinner in the host's home becomes a scene of confrontation and conflict between the host and his guest. Shared meals in general, as described by Ruchama Weiss, are vehicles of social interaction: The relationships that are expressed at meals are "an encrypted language for complex relationships between diners, relationships that combine, on one hand, love and desire to provide with, on

---

4 In Barthes's terms, bread types are social markers, though nowadays they have been reversed. Black bread is considered better quality and more nutritious and is priced higher than white bread (Barthes 1961, 980). On challah and its place in Eastern Europe, see Marks 2010, 96–101; Ginsberg 2011, 23. On black bread, the "bread of the poor" of the Jews of Eastern Europe, see Ginsberg 2011, 56.

the other, competition, personal-political struggles, and a will to control" (Weiss 2010, 20).

Despite the fact that both men diverge from the accepted rules of behavior, it seems that the narrator is in favor of the poor man. When the miserly rich man claims that challah is more expensive than regular bread, the poor man replies in a clever and defiant manner that there is justification for the challah's high cost. The audience listening to the story may identify with the poor man and get satisfaction from the rich one being "tricked," but it cannot ignore the criticism of the poor man's gluttony.

Poor Man's Beans

IFA 12582

Told by Camelia Shahar-Russo, Turkey
Recorded by Tamar Alexander

Once there was a very rich man who got sick and tired of eating delicacies. He said: "I want to try and eat poor man's beans. I want to taste what they eat."

The rich man told the maid: "This week, I want you to cook me poor man's beans. I want to know what beans are."

At the rich man's house there was in abundance meat, oil, and onions. The maid cooked him a delicious bean soup, with plenty of meat, onions, oil and tomato sauce, all the world's best ingredients.

The rich man ate the soup. Excited, he said: "Poor people are real rascals! They say that beans are poor man's food but see how tasty and delicious this dish is!"

After some time, the rich man told the maid: "Prepare me once again poor man's beans."

The maid thought: "This time I will teach him a lesson and show him what poor man's beans really are."

She took just a small piece of onion and a drop of oil, as oil is expensive. Therefore, the onion burnt. She did not put any meat but a few bones; she added a drop of tomato sauce and cooked the dish.

The rich man said: "What kind of dish did you prepare this time? It has no taste at all."

"You see," said the maid, "this is real poor man's beans, not like what I made you before."

Discussion of
"POOR MAN'S BEANS"

I
n IFA, there is no biographical information about the storyteller, Camelia Shahar-Russo, except that fifteen tales are registered in her name at IFA. This tale was filed in the archives in 1979.

Food, being an essential part of human life, also serves as a means to characterize social status and to differentiate between classes in society. The upper classes use food to distinguish themselves from members of the lower classes. This is reflected both in types of food and eating methods (Counihan 1999, 8) and in taste, defined usually by the upper class (Bourdieu 1984).

The tale under discussion focuses on this issue. The food that stands at the center of the discussion and serves as a marker for economic status is the bean stew described as food of the poor.[1] This identification has been rooted in culture for many generations (Roden 1980, 189). But in Turkey, the country of origin of the narrator, beans are called the "Sultan of the common man's kitchen" and are also considered its national food.[2] Among Spanish communities too, beans were a popular and loved food (Marks 2010, 43).

---

1 On the origin and spread of beans in the Western world, see Albala 2007, chap. 9, 127–90.

2 See Jolanda Thijssen, "Kuru Fasulye (Turkish White Bean Stew)," Veganevergreens, accessed December 28, 2020, https://veganevergreens.world/turkish-kuru-fasulye/; and Elizabeth Taviloglu, "Turkish Beans: Pinto Beans in Olive Oil," Spruce Eats, September 10, 2019, http://turkishfood.about.com/od/BeansRiceGrains/r/Navy-Bean-Stew-Considered-Turkey-S-National-Dish.htm.

It seems that the narrator expresses support for the poor, and places in a dichotomous way the image of the maid as opposed to the image of the rich man. The rich man is portrayed as a hedonist who is bored with the abundant dishes on his table, indifferent to the suffering of the poor, and even doubting their distress.

His request to taste poor people's beans can be interpreted as a gesture of empathy and a process of becoming familiar with another person's predicament. It would have been possible to hope that in the wake of this "class visit," the rich man would have been willing to help the poor. But his request is presented in the tale in a negative light, as a repulsive whim intended to vary his menu and dispel his boredom.

The maid apparently belongs to the poor class. In her naïveté, and perhaps in her kindness, she seeks to shield her master from the bitter taste of poverty food. So she cooks him a bowl of beans from fine ingredients and produces a rich and delicious dish. The rich man enjoys the taste of the dish, but displays imperviousness and malice when he claims that the poor complain unjustly and calls them "rascals." Then the maid, who knows very well what a poor person's dish is, prepares beans for him once more, and this time she does not use expensive ingredients as before.[3] The taste is indeed different, and the rich man is exposed to an untasty dish that is truly the lot of the poor.

As stated by Eve Jochnowitz: "The palate is part of the mouth but is also understood as a socially constructed site; that is geographically specific, and possibly even gender-and class-specific" (2015, 307).

The tale positions the two characters as representatives of the two economic classes in society, the rich and the poor. The status of the poor is represented by a woman who, in a patriarchal society, is inferior first of all just because of her gender, and therefore her image emphasizes the inferiority of

---

3 In Tamar Alexander's view, this tale confronts the foolish behavior of the rich with the clever behavior of the maid, and therefore she associates it with the international tale type AT 920–929 Clever Acts and Words (Alexander and Noy1989, 279).

poor people. The maid's desire to placate and make her master's life easier seems to reflect the conduct of the poor. Members of this class carry out unpleasant actions for the rich, thus making the latter's life easier. The rich man, for his part, represents the ugliness that characterizes the members of his class for their insensitivity, lack of faith, and ignorance of the situation of other people.

The distinction between rich and poor in our tale focuses not only on the food itself but also on the way it is prepared. When the maid cooks the beans as the poor do in their kitchens, the ingredients that make up the dish are limited and few, resulting in a dish that, in the eyes of the rich man, is inedible. The food in this tale thus makes tangible the gulf between rich and poor.

The Way to Become Rich

IFA 16648

Told and recorded by Shimon
Kbarnit Likbornik, Russia

I n a small town lived a Jewish man and his family. His trade was to act as a middleman. In fact, he had very little success in providing for his family. There were times when at home there was not even bread for the children.

His friend, a Hasid, told him once during a talk that he should visit the rebbe, the tzadik (literally "the righteous one"): "Without any doubt, your salvation will come from the rebbe." And he said, "You should know that the tzadik is a part of Divination above, and he has the power to bring down *Shefah* (abundance)—from the celestial spheres. And even more, the tzadik knows the future, and there is nothing he is unable to do. If God sentences a decree on someone, the tzadik has the power to cancel it, as it happened with Abraham the Patriarch. God sentenced Sodom to doom, and Abraham wanted to cancel the decree.

"He who believes in the tzadik's sayings and always sees them as great wonders, later discovers that all that has happened was already hinted in these sayings."

The Jewish man listened to his friend and went to the rebbe. He brought him as a gift the last coins he had. He complained to the rebbe that he was born five minutes too late. The rebbe asked him for an explanation. "Everywhere I go to propose some deal, they tell me: too bad, if you would have come five minutes earlier, we would have bought from you. In the meantime we bought already and we don't need anymore," said the man.

The rebbe blessed him with profuse blessings and good livelihood.

Thus, it repeated itself every time he visited the rebbe, but his livelihood did not improve at all.

When the situation became unbearable, his wife told him, "Do you think the rebbe will change your luck and bring you wealth on a silver platter, if you do not demand it from him sternly? As long as you are silent, the rebbe does not know your real situation. How much longer can the children and we suffer and starve? Go to the rebbe and do not leave until he promises you that soon you will become rich!"

The man traveled to the rebbe. He told him about his troubles: there is no bread at home, his children are pale from starvation, the situation is unbearable and it is impossible to continue this suffering.

"I am begging the rebbe to please cancel the decree God sentenced for me, to always suffer from hunger. As all know it, God sentences and the tzadik cancels. I cannot and will not move from here until the rebbe will promise me that soon I will become rich."

The rebbe talked to his heart, telling him to trust in God who will provide for him. Nevertheless, the man continued claiming, "I will not go out of here without a promise that I will become rich."

"Well," said the Rebbe, "listen carefully to what I am about to tell you, and if you will fulfill every detail as I order you, you will become rich."

"I will do anything," replied the man.

"Go back home and God will bring you success and you will earn some money. You will use all this money, to the last coin, to buy wine, challah, fish, meat, prunes, and tasty cakes. Do not let anyone touch anything. You yourself will prepare everything. You will cook. Then bring everything to the table. Put on your best Shabbat clothes and sit by yourself at the table, drink wine, and eat the good food you prepared. Do not let anyone of your household come to the table and touch the dishes, even the crumbs on the floor. You have to eat everything alone."

The man returned home in good spirits. Easily he earned some money and started to carry out the rebbe's orders. He bought everything. He prepared everything by himself. He himself cooked. His wife asked him, "What is the special occasion?"

"The rebbe orders so," he replied. His wife looked and waited patiently.

Once he was done, he put everything on the table, put on his best Shabbat clothes and sat at the table. He drank wine and started eating. His wife approached the table and he cruelly sent her away. She started crying and yelled, "Shmuel, what did the rebbe do to you? He stole your golden heart and gave you a stone one instead? How can the rebbe be so cruel? If not for me, at least do for your starving children!"

She asked him to at least give some of this meal to the children, but he refused and continued to eat. One child dared to approach, asked and begged him, "Daddy, give me a piece of challah, a small piece like my finger!" But he refused. Another child approached: "Daddy, give me a tiny piece, a little bit of meat." He refused. A third one drew near: "Daddy, give me only the bone to chew on, just the bone." He refused. The fourth child came close to him and caressed him: "Daddy, just let me pick up the crumb from the floor!" He refused.

Seeing that, his wife cried out aloud and all the children joined her. The food started to get stuck in his throat, but he held on. At last, his youngest daughter approached him. She kissed him and said, "Daddy, I always love you and you love me too, isn't it so Daddy? Give me food. My mouth is so hungry. Give me whatever you want, but give me food."

That is when he broke down. He stood up, broke into tears and yelled in a pitiful voice, "God, just give me bread to eat and cloth to wear!" Then he screamed in a horrified voice, "I do not want to be rich. Do you hear me rebbe? I do not want to be rich."

He invited his wife and children to the table, to eat together with him, and he let slip in a relieved cry, "If this is the way to become rich, I cannot and do not want to be rich."

Discussion of
"THE WAY TO BECOME RICH"

T here is no information about the storyteller, Shimon Kbarnit Lik-
bornik, except that twenty-eight tales are registered in his name
at IFA. This tale was filed in the archives in 1988.

This tale criticizes the economic status of rich people in society. It represents
them as selfish, ruthless, and impervious to the needs of others, even members
of their own household. According to this tale, lower-class people are actually morally superior. The tale thus justifies, indeed in a strange way, social
stratification, and encourages a sense of pride in belonging to the lower class.

The tale combines in its plot the way of life of Eastern European Jews
generally and Hasidic society more particularly. It is structured as a kind
of Hasidic tale: A poor wretched man whose trade as a middleman cannot
support his family.[1] He asks to change his financial situation so he can feed
his hungry children. He accepts the advice of his Hasidic friend and turns
to the rebbe, the tzadik (literally "the righteous one").

The narrator offers in brief, by means of the protagonist's friend, the main
principles of the Hasidic doctrine of the tzadik:[2]

- The tzadik is "part of God above."
- The tzadik brings down abundance from the upper worlds to the
  lower world.

---

1 On the difficult economic situation of most East European Jews, including
   the middlemen who constituted 18 percent of the Jewish professions at the end
   of the nineteenth century, see Tartakower 1964.
2 For more on the theory of the tzadik in Hasidism and its expression in tales, see
   Dvir-Goldberg, 2003.

- The tzadik knows people's fates.
- The tzadik can do anything.
- The tzadik can nullify God's decree, as Abraham our father wanted to do with Sodom.
- The words of the tzadik can perform miracles.

The Hasidic friend compares the tzadik's ability to nullify a decree from Heaven to Abraham the Patriarch and his actions concerning Sodom.[3]

The narrator does not dwell on this parallel, but it has interesting connotations for the topic of the tale. In rabbinical sources, the sin of the people of Sodom is sometimes explained by their unwillingness to share their property with others. For example: "There are four types of character in people: 1) One that says, 'Mine is mine, and yours is yours'. This is a commonplace type; some say this is a Sodom-type of character. 2) One that says, 'Mine is yours and yours is mine', is an unlearned person. 3) One that says, 'Mine is yours and yours is yours', is a pious person. 4) One that says, 'Mine is mine, and yours is mine', is a wicked person" (Mishnah Avot 5:10). In another source, the Sodomites are described as reluctant to share their food: "The Sodomites said as food is coming out of our land and silver and gold are coming out of our land and precious stones and gems are coming out of our land we do not need people to come to us for they are coming to take from us" (Tosefta Sotah [Lieberman] 3:12).

---

3 Regarding Abraham defending Sodom, see, for example, Bereshit Rabbah 39:6: "R. Azariah in R. Aha's name referred the verse to Abraham our father. When Abraham our father stood to plead for mercy for the Sodomites, what is written there? (Gen. 18:25): 'That be far from thee to do after this manner, to slay the righteous with the wicked: and that the righteous should be as the wicked, that be far from thee: Shall not the Judge of all the earth do right?'"; Midrash Tanhuma, Vayar 8: "After the Sodomites had transgressed, He revealed His intentions to Abraham in order to discover something to their credit, as it is said: 'And the Lord said: Shall I hide from Abraham?' Abraham began to plead in their behalf, as it is said (Gen. 18:23): 'And Abraham drew near, and said, Wilt thou also destroy the righteous with the wicked?'" *Drew near* is an expression used to indicate prayer.

In the tale, the rebbe refrains from giving concrete advice to the poor man: he wishes to strengthen his faith and make him accept his difficult financial situation. In retrospect, the rebbe's behavior is understandable, since the desire to be wealthy has a very burdensome price. After the poor man turns to the rebbe several times, insisting that he remove him from his financial distress, the rebbe finally reveals to him the way to get rich. This discovery is not a miraculous or supernatural kind of knowledge but rather a very cruel, realistic behavior: to eat all the delicacies he has acquired without sharing them with his family.

According to the narrator's view, wealth is not just an economic condition but a collection of traits. Who is rich? The one who is able to completely ignore the distress of others, even the ones closest to him.

The poor man's wife is mentioned four times in the tale. When presented for the first time, we are introduced to her skepticism about the rebbe's abilities. The wife, unlike her husband, does not attribute hidden knowledge to the rebbe and believes he knows nothing of their predicament. Therefore, she urges her husband to act forcefully and to demand a solution from the rebbe. She then attributes her husband's selfish actions to the rebbe's failure, which she says has changed the character of her husband: "He stole your golden heart and gave you a stone one instead."

The wife's false impressions ultimately come to enhance the image of the rebbe, after the real motives underlying his advice for lack of action and apparent errors are revealed.

The wife is mentioned two times more, but unlike the previous descriptions, she is not defiant but submissive and weak while exposed to her husband's selfishness in eating alone and refusing to share his meal with her.

The most difficult picture, described in the tale in seven stages, is the plea to the father, by each member of the family for a little food: his wife waits for him to share his meal with her, then cries and asks him to feed his children. Then their five children turn to him one by one. Every child turns to him asking for a smaller amount of food than the previous one did (a small piece of challah, some meat, a bone to lick, a crumb that fell on the floor). The pleas of the hungry children tear at his heart, but the father expels every child with their request each time. The only one who succeeds in getting the father out of his selfishness and cruelty is his young daughter. The special bond between her and her father is disclosed in her plea, perhaps because she is the only girl among the sons and the youngest of them all. It is possible that the love that prevails between them, her kiss, and the manner in which she turns to him in fact cause his change of heart.[4] She does not ask for a specific portion of the meal, but reminds him of his duty as the father of the family: "Give me food. My mouth is so hungry. Give me whatever you want, but give me food."

In the end, the father is no longer able to withstand the distress of his family and shares with them the succulent dishes. In so doing, he renounces the opportunity of becoming wealthy, for its price is emotionally unbearable to him. The tale leads the audience to the conclusion that it is preferable to remain poor than to be heartlessly rich. By representing the meal and the hungry persons around it, the tale evokes a sympathetic response; the description touches everyone and is understood by all. The tale then creates a correlation between economic status and morality. The consolation presented at the end preserves the society's economic stratification and class structure. The message is very clear: better to be poor, generous, and sensitive than to be rich, stingy, and heartless.

---

4 In many of the folktales, the youngest son, who is the weakest link in the family, succeeds in the task (see, for example, "The King and His Three Sons" [IFA 545]). For more information see Luthi 1970, 142.

THE PRICE OF SMELLING

IFA 178

TOLD BY SA'ID KAFIA, YEMEN
RECORDED BY YIHIA YIHIA

It is told that there was a poor man who could not provide for himself and lived from alms the townspeople gave him. One day a woman gave him half a loaf of bread. The poor man sat in the shade of a house, which from its window disseminated the fragrance of cooked food. The poor man ate the bread and smelled the dish's fragrance until he was satiated. In the meantime the landlord, a very rich and miserly man, came out. The poor man stood up and thanked him for the excellent dish's smell.

The rich man replied grudgingly, "You enjoyed it? Pay me for smelling my dish."

The poor man told him, "No way! Did I eat from your dish that I have to pay for it? I just smelled it and nothing more."

The rich man sued the poor man in court. The judge heard the arguments of both sides and told the poor man, "Pay him a penny!"

The poor man answered, "I do not have even one penny."

The judge postponed the trial to the next day, so the poor man, in the meantime, could get a loan of one penny. The poor man went, pawned his shirt, and borrowed the money. The next day, both of them came to the judge, and the poor man gave him the penny.

The judge summoned the rich man, who thought that he would immediately get the penny. The judge hit the stone floor with the coin and asked him, "What did you hear, rich man?"

He replied, "A chime."

The judge ruled wisely, "You heard the chime of the penny, the poor man smelled your dish. The chime is your payment and the penny is returned to the poor man."

Discussion of
"The Price of Smelling"

There is no biographical information about the storyteller, Sa'id Kafia, in the archives. This is the only tale registered in his name at IFA. It was filed in 1957 and is one of the first to be recorded by IFA. It belongs to the international tale type AT 1804B, ATU 1804B, Payment with the Clink of Money. At IFA, there are ten other versions of the tale recorded over several decades.[1]

The tale describes a confrontation between a poor, destitute man and a rich, heartless one. It clearly favors the poor man, whose only livelihood depends on the generosity and compassion of the community. His food is supplied to him by others, he finds refuge from the heat of the day in the shadow cast from one of the houses, and he wants to enjoy the smell of a fragrant dish. As a destitute man, he eats the most basic food—bread—and the other pleasures of life are supplied to him in using his imagination: the smell of stew instead of its taste, the shadow of a house instead of a shaded room. His imagination allows him to eat and be satiated, chewing the bread and imagining the dish whose smell he inhales.

Smells affect us even when we are not aware of it. They provoke strong emotional reactions, bring back memories, and connect us to past experiences and the emotional world related to these experiences (Classen 1994, 1–2).

Through the tale's description of the poor, hungry man smelling the fragrant dish, the audience understands and senses his experience, the yearning

---

1 The additional versions are IFA 8990—Morocco; IFA 6123 and 6498—Greece; IFA 8481—Israel, Sephardic; IFA 1779—Israel, Ashkenazic; IFA 9351—Israel, Arab; IFA 5929—Kurdistan Iraq; IFA 5690, 6792, and 9176—Iraq.

and the unsatisfied hunger aroused by the dish's aroma. It is, of course, impossible to store or retain the smells that waft through the air. Therefore, when we hear the rich man's demand for a smeller's fee, the injustice strikes us as outrageous. It contradicts not only our values and beliefs but also the inner sensory world of each one of us. In this case, too, there is no need to elaborate on the injustice, for everyone who hears the rich man's absurd demand feels appalled by it.

These feelings are intensified when it seems that the judge does not understand the poor man's distress and requires him to obtain a coin. The tale tells that the poor man had to pawn his very shirt to obtain the required coin. This act simultaneously raises a wide spectrum of feelings. It deepens our pity for the hungry poor, our loathing for the rich, and our indignation at the judicial establishment that is supposed to deliver justice in society.

At the end of the tale, the judge cleverly compares two abstract concepts—smell and sound—and this comparison is received with complete surprise and even adds an amusing tone to the drama that has taken place so far. All's well that ends well: the poor man gets his coin back, the rich man receives no reward, and the judge acts in the name of justice.

This tale conjures up in a most painful way the social injustices that exist in reality. But it also corrects them in the world of imagination. There wrong and injustice are eliminated, giving rise to hope and comfort.

4

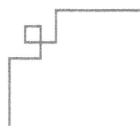

IT IS KOSHER
AND FIT TO EAT

FOOD AND KASHRUT

Food is a powerful means whereby people associate themselves with a particular group and differentiate themselves from the "other" (Brulotte and Di Giovane 2014; Counihan 1999; Feeley-Harnik 1981; Fischler 1988; Goode 1992; Long 2015; Mintz 2002). Occasionally, foods of one group are perceived as repulsive and uneatable by a different group (Jones 2000). A widely known example is how the English identify the French as "frog eaters" (Fischler 1988, 280) and are shocked by their consumption of horse meat. The Western world in general recoils from foreign diets that include the consumption of dogs, rodents, reptiles, and insects.

Traditional Jewish culture places severe and detailed restrictions on food that define what is kosher—that is, suitable and proper for consumption by Jews—and nonkosher, unsuitable and therefore forbidden. These restrictions, called *kashrut*, relate to various issues:

1. The types of animals permitted and forbidden to eat (according to the biblical rulings in Leviticus 11 and Deuteronomy 22). Among the forbidden, pork is perhaps the best known (Rosenblum 2010b).

2. The methods of slaughtering animals and determining whether their meat is edible or not, as well as ways to prepare meat by salting and removing its blood. These are mentioned in the Torah as general instructions (Genesis 32:33; Exodus 22:30; Leviticus 17:13–14, 22:28; Deuteronomy 12:20–24, 14:21). Detailed instructions were later elaborated (Mishnah Chulin; Babylonian Talmud Chulin; Maimonides' *Mishneh Torah*, Laws of Slaughter; Shulchan Arukh, Yoreh De'ah).

3. The various ways of cooking and eating, particularly regarding the complete separation between meat and milk. This is a must, and requires separate utensils while cooking, separate serving dishes, and the restriction of every meal to one or the other but not both. This custom is based on the Torah's instruction, repeated three times, exactly in the same language: "Thou shalt not seethe a kid in his mother's milk" (Exodus 23:19; 34:26; Deuteronomy 14:21).

Jewish thought and modern research have attempted to provide various reasons for these limitations.[2] Several medieval philosophers explained kashrut as a means of maintaining health and hygiene. For example, R. Shmuel ben Meir (Rashbam), who lived in France in the years 1040–1105, argued that nonkosher animals are harmful to health: "All beasts and animals and birds and fish and species of locusts and vermin that the Holy One blessed be he has forbidden to Israel are abominable and spoil and heat the body, and therefore they are called impure. And even prominent doctors say so" (Commentary on Leviticus 11:3).

R. Moshe ben Nachman (Ramban, Spanish, 1194–1270) explained the difference between kosher and unkosher fish. Kosher fish, bearing fins and scales, dwell in clear water and are safe for consumption. Unkosher ones (lacking fins and scales) dwell in murky water and are dangerous to eat:

---

2 See Cooper 1993: 17–36; Segal 2014.

The reason for the existence of fins and scales is because their bearers always dwell in the upper clear water and receive an increase of air that enters there. Therefore, they have a small amount of heat which expels the phlegm, like the function of wool and hair and nails in man and beast. And those which have no fins and scales will always dwell in the bottom of the water in their murkiness, and for the most part the humidity and the heat would not reject anything. And therefore they have cold phlegm close to death, and it is deadly in some waters like in stale lakes. (Commentary on Leviticus 11:9)

R. Moshe ben Maimon (Maimonides, Spanish, 1135–1204) explained that the prohibition against eating pork is due to its filth:

The principal reason why the Law forbids swine's flesh is to be found in the circumstance that its habits and its food are very dirty and loathsome. It has already been pointed out how emphatically the Law enjoins the removal of the sight of loathsome objects, even in the field and in the camp; how much more objectionable is such a sight in towns. But if it were allowed to eat swine's flesh, the streets and houses would be more dirty than any cesspool, as may be seen at present in the country of the Franks. (*Guide for the Perplexed*, part 3, chapter 48, in M. Friedlander 1904, 370–71)

Other interpretations of kashrut pointed out an ethical aspect. For example, R. Abraham Ibn Ezra (Spanish, 1089–1167) perceived the cooking of meat in milk as a cruel act and explained its prohibition in this context:

We have no need to ask the reason for his prohibition, for it is hidden from the eyes of the wise. Perhaps it was cruel to cook the goat with his mother's milk, as it is mentioned in Leviticus 22:28: "And whether it be cow, or ewe, ye shall not kill it and her young both in one day." And also in Deuteronomy 22:6: "If a bird's nest chance to be before thee in the way in any tree, or on the ground, whether they be young ones, or eggs, and the dame sitting upon the young, or upon the eggs, thou shalt not take the dame with the young." (Commentary on Exodus 23:19)

Some modern researchers have explained the prohibition of eating pork as based on economic reasons: in the Middle East, the pig, being an omnivore, competes with humans for the same scarce edible resources. By banning its meat, the pig is removed from this geographic area, securing food for humans (Harris 1975; 1987).

Another modern researcher explains the whole concept of kashrut, as described in the Bible, as intending to create a clear categorization, albeit arbitrary, of the animal world (Douglas 1966, 1997). Kosher animals are the ones that bear the traits characteristic of a defined space (air, earth, water). Nonkosher animals are the ones lacking these traits or bearing traits fitting two defined spaces. For example, nonkosher crustaceans live in water but walk like creatures on earth.

Another reason offered to explain kashrut was the desire to separate from surrounding cultures. Various modern researchers have proposed this explanation (Diner 2002; Fischler 1988; Goldstein 2018, 47; Kraemer 2007; Rosenblum 2010a, 2010b), but it can also be found in earlier traditions. For example, this is one of the reasons given for the prohibition of pork:

"And ye shall be holy unto me: for I the Lord am holy . . ." (Leviticus 20:26), just as I am holy so you should be holy, as I separate myself so you should separate, "and have severed you from other people, that ye should be mine . . ." (Leviticus 20:26). If you are separated from the nations, you are mine. And if not, you belong to Nebuchadnezzar king of Babylon and his companions. Rabbi Elazar ben Azariah said: How do we learn it? One should not say it is impossible to eat pork . . . but it is possible. But what shall I do? My Father in heaven hath decreed me. (Sifra Kedoshim 19:22; Yalkut Shimoni Torah, *Parashat Kedoshim* 247)

The same idea is also offered to explain the separation between meat and milk:

> Meat boiled in milk is undoubtedly gross food, and makes overfull; but I think that most probably it is also prohibited because it is somehow connected with idolatry, forming perhaps part of the service, or being used on some festival of the heathen. I find a support for this view in the circumstance that the Law mentions the prohibition twice after the commandment given concerning the festivals: "Three times in the year all thy males shall appear before the Lord God" (Exodus 23:17 and 34:23) as if to say "When you come before me on you festivals, do not seethe your food in the manner as the heathen used to do." This I consider as the best reason for the prohibition. (Maimonides, *Guide to the Perplexed*, part 3, chap. 48, in M. Friedlander 1904, 371)

Whatever the reason, the result of these restrictions is singular and succinct: a very clear definition of Jewish identity. As Lisa Hess mentions, "Kashrut is a path of belonging" (Hess 2012: 330), but she also points out the dangerous aspect of it: "Kashrut can be used as a weapon of tribal exclusion" (2012, 333). Joëlle Bahloul in her study of the Algerian Jews living in France suggests that eating kosher meat establishes a deep connection between the individual and the community (1983, 208). Susan Sered regards kashrut as a means of group definition: "Kashrut must be understood as contributing to the definition of the Jewish community, the extended network of kin, the multigenerational web of human beings with which one is connected with bonds of reciprocal care and responsibility" (Sered 1992, 90).

This Jewish identity is achieved in two ways: one is through the designation of foods permitted for consumption and foods forbidden for consumption. The stipulations have their effect even if, sometimes, the laws' details are not uniform and can be interpreted variously. Disputes do exist between rabbinical courts regarding how to render kosher various food products, but there is agreement, nevertheless, on most issues related to kashrut. The second way is accomplished by separating Jews from the "others" and preventing any possibility of a Jew dining at gentiles' tables or eating their food. References to the refusal to eat the food of non-Jews appear already in writings that can be attributed to the Babylonian exile and the Second Temple period, such as the Book of Daniel 1:8; Book of Tobit 1; Book of Jubilees 22:23; and Sefer Yehudit 12, 1–2 (Kraemer 2007, 26–28).

In folk literature, three main types of nonkosher food are presented: 1) meat that has not been slaughtered or prepared properly, 2) meat that is forbidden to eat (mostly pork), and 3) meat mixed with milk. In the IFA's folktales, there is a complex and sometimes ambivalent attitude toward kashrut, perhaps due to the fact that when the tales were recorded, many Jews no longer observed it.

The tales describe the economic price and even the financial and social damage that the observance of kashrut laws entails. For example, in the tale "Converted to Irritate," the reason for the conversion of all the Jews in the city is expressed in their anger at the fact that all the cows (eight or ten according to the narrator) were bought and slaughtered before Pesach and were deemed unfit to be eaten: "They did not want to stay Jewish anymore. And all of this because the cows were unfit for eating" (IFA 14627).

The tales ironically describe the meticulousness required in the observance of kashrut rules. For example, "The Jewish Hunter in the Indian Reserve" describes a Jewish hunter who, despite the many days he spent tracking a buffalo, at the last minute gave up the hunt because by mistake he took the wrong tomahawk, which was reserved for milk (IFA 9389).

Some of the tales present, with indulgence, the nonobservance of kashrut. For example, "The Tasty Nuts" describes how a Jew ate especially tasty nuts for years. And when it finally turns out that they were fried in pork fat, he is now careful to eat only nuts that were fried on coals, to make sure there is no suspicion of any fat on them (IFA 5092).

However, the tales also express pride in the ability to keep kosher and stand firm against the temptations of the gentile's kitchen.

This chapter contains six tales. The first four deal with the problems that arise when meals are shared by Jews and gentiles. The last two tales deal with kashrut issues within the Jewish kitchen.

If Only You Knew the Taste

IFA 20195

Told by Shela Aranya, Turkey
Recorded by Matilda Coen-Sarano

A new rabbi arrived in a village. The local priest wanted to honor the "rabbi of the Jews" and invited him one evening to eat at his house.

The rabbi, of course, could not share the meal, for the food was not kosher, but he did not want to insult the priest, which certainly is improper.

The priest set a very nice table, seated the rabbi with great respect and said to him: "Rabbi, please, eat."

The rabbi said: "I cannot eat!"

"Why can't you?"

"Because our Torah does not allow us."

"If only you knew the taste!" said the priest, handing him another plate. Again, the rabbi, unable to eat, said to him: "No! No! I cannot eat! Our holy Torah does not allow us."

For each portion, the priest repeated over and over: "Ah! If only you knew the taste! If only you knew the taste!"

The rabbi began to get annoyed. As soon as he was about to leave, the rabbi said to the priest: "Most thanks! You have done me a great honor. It is a pity I did not eat, but the table was set beautifully, and the food looked very tasty too! Give my thanks to your wife who treated me with so much respect."

"Ah!" the priest said to him, "We priests cannot marry! Our Torah does not allow us!"

"Ah! If only you knew the taste!" said the rabbi.

Discussion of
"If Only You Knew the Taste"

The storyteller, Shela Aranya, was born in Istanbul, Turkey. This is the only tale registered in her name at IFA. It was filed in the archives in 1995.

This tale belongs to the international type ATU 1855D, You Do Not Know What You Are Missing: A priest rides in a train eating a ham sandwich. He offers one to a rabbi (Jew) sitting across from him. The rabbi explains that he is not allowed to eat pork. The clergyman says: "You don't know what you are missing—pork is very good." When the clergyman leaves the train, the rabbi says: "Greetings to you wife." The clergyman answers that he is not allowed to marry. The rabbi replies, "You don't know what you are missing—women are very good." At IFA eleven versions of this tale are registered.[1]

This tale deals with an encounter between official representatives of two religions: a Jewish rabbi and a Christian priest. The exposition at the beginning of the tale presents an idyllic picture. The village priest invites the newcomer rabbi to dine at his home. His hospitality is impeccable. The table is set with abundant delicacies. The rabbi is invited with great respect to taste them. The communal meal has a social significance of brotherhood and cooperation (Julier 2013; Kraemer 2007, 28; Weiss 2010).

---

1 There are six versions from Poland: IFA 2551, IFA 6358, IFA 6705, IFA 13030, IFA 15907, IFA 16199. One version is from Russia: IFA 7399. Three versions are from Turkey: IFA 12574, IFA 20266, IFA 21269. Tamar Alexander and Noy discusses IFA 12574 (1989, 277). Alexander also refers in general to the religious conflict that arises from all three versions (1999, 374–75). One version is from Spain: IFA 10351. In the past, these tales have been ascribed to the general oicotype AT *1873, Confrontation between Jew and Christian.

Precisely at this point—which is a climax of closeness and trust—the conflict is about to be revealed in its full force because the rules of kashrut do not allow for joint eating.

This description resonates with one of another meal that cannot be shared. This is Aesop's fable (seventh century BCE) of the Stork and the Fox, common throughout the world. Its tale type is AT 60, Fox and Crane Invite Each Other. The fable tells of a stork and a fox, two bitter enemies, who host each other in turn for a communal meal. Despite the neighborly gesture, each of them maliciously and deliberately serves the food in a dish that the guest cannot eat from. Each time only the host gets to eat, while the guest remains hungry. The anger and frustration of the hungry guest are channeled into revenge resolved by a reciprocal invitation.

Our tale does not describe the priest's feelings in light of his guest's refusal to eat from the multitude of foods he prepared for him. However, the audience may well imagine, for the feelings of disappointment, indignation, and anger may arise in any frustrated host.[2] The rabbi's refusal to share the meal can be interpreted by the priest as reluctance to cooperate while turning a back on his attempt at a rapprochement. Thus the tale exposes the social price of Jewish separateness, and offers an additional interpretation for the next part of the plot.

On the visible level criticism is directed at the priest. At first, criticism can be inferred from the story's setting: the village. It is reasonable to assume that the inhabitants are not numerous, and they can easily be recognized. Therefore, the priest would know the way of life of the Jews living in that village and be aware of kashrut issues. In order to remove any doubt about the priest's ignorance of Jewish law, it is mentioned that the

---

2 Haya Bar-Itzhak writes about the sensitive and charged relationships between a guest and his host: "The host does a good turn for the guest, welcoming him into his house, and expects that the latter will display gratitude. Such relations frequently lead to a situation in which the host, feeling his power, pressures his guest and exploits him to his own benefit or places him at risk against his will" (2001, 107).

Jewish rabbi explained to his host the reason for his inability to eat with him. Now the priest may be expected, as a clergyman, to stop the meal and apologize to the rabbi. But as the plot unfolds, it seems that the priest acts as a representative of the Christian religion that persecutes Judaism. He abuses his guest; he continues to urge him to taste the dishes he is served and breaches the basic laws of hospitality when he is the only one who eats. The provocation culminates when after each dish the priest savors, he repeatedly mentions the taste the rabbi is missing. The listeners, who see themselves as participants in the observance of kashrut laws, identify with the rabbi and experience the insult as he does. But on a deeper level the situation presented can be interpreted not as a religious conflict specifically but as a universal human event of a hurt host seeking to retaliate and harm the guest who rejected his invitation. This offense is reminiscent of a talmudic narrative about the founding of Christianity, which is explained as a case of hurt feelings when Jesus was insulted by the attitude of his master Joshua ben Perahiah (Sanhedrin 107b).

Again, most visibly, the balance is restored when the rabbi behaves like the priest. He follows the rules of courtesy, expressing appreciation for the honor he received, wishing he could eat, praising the sight of the table and the delicacies served. Finally, demonstrating ignorance and naïveté of the laws concerning the clergy's celibacy, he wishes to thank the priest's wife. After the priest answers that he has no wife and presents his celibacy as a religious imperative, the rabbi can finally reply to the priest in the same language, "If only you knew the taste."[3] The rabbi's wisdom is revealed at the end of the tale and the Jewish audience's lost honor is returned after their food laws were ridiculed.

---

3 On the close connection between food and conjugal relationships, see chapter 2.

THE JEWISH RABBI AND THE KING

IFA 6110

TOLD BY DAVID PEREZ, MOROCCO
RECORDED BY YIHIA PEREZ

A king wanted to put the rabbi of the Jews of his town to a test and said to him: "Rabbi, bring your wife to my palace, I will assign her a room and there she will cook the dishes for lunch, because I want you to eat today at my table."

The rabbi accepted the king's proposal and brought his wife to the palace where she received an assigned room. She decided to prepare couscous (a special Moroccan dish made of dough bits with vegetables and meat) for the rabbi.

The king told one of his servants: "Go and see what the rabbi's wife is doing and tell the cook to do the same."

And so it was. The rabbi's wife prepared the dough bits, and the chef in his kitchen prepared the dough bits too. She prepared the vegetables, and the chef prepared them too. She prepared the meat in a certain way, and he also prepared it in the same way. When the rabbi's wife finished cooking, she put the dish on a special plate. The chef served his dish on an identical plate. After he finished he served the stew to the king. The King hid the plate in the dining room. It was time for the meal and the wife served the couscous dish to the rabbi. The king then told the rabbi: "Before you begin with the meal, just take off your cloak."

The rabbi accepted the decree and removed the cloak over his head. While his face was covered with the cloak the king replaced the rabbi's plate (which was kosher for eating) with the plate prepared by his cook (which was forbidden to eat because a gentile prepared it and the meat was not kosher).

They sat down to eat. The king expected that the rabbi would begin the meal but he did not begin. The king asked him why. The rabbi replied:

"My parents taught me that once my eyes were covered and I could not see anything, I should not eat the food that was served before me for fear of wrongdoing."

The king was dumbfounded and thanked God for the rabbi's wisdom. From that day on, he converted to Judaism and with him his whole kingdom.

Discussion of
"The Jewish Rabbi and the King"

The storyteller, David Perez, was born in 1923 in the small town of Boujad, Morocco, situated at 32°46′N, 6°24′W. He immigrated to Israel in 1956. Twenty-four of his tales are registered at IFA, all of them recorded by his son, Yihia Perez. This tale was filed in the archives in 1964.

This tale reflects the mistrust and mutual suspicion accompanying an encounter between Jews and gentiles. This issue is reflected in the plot through the description of food preparation and its consumption. The tale expresses the constant sense of danger that lurks when a Jew sits at a gentile's table and his fear of being served unfit food for him to eat if he does not stand on his guard and, literally, keep his eyes open the whole time.

The plot starts by giving information about the imminent threat—exposing the Jewish rabbi to temptation. This information, hidden from the tale's characters, except for the king, creates tension that extends throughout the story. Allegedly, the rabbi is accorded great respect—he is invited to dine at the king's table. It seems that the king also respects Jewish tradition and knows the principles of kashrut. He ensures that the rabbi will eat kosher food cooked by his wife in a special space allotted her in the palace. Later on, the other characters in the story seem to think that the king is even more respectful when he asks his cook to prepare the exact same dish as the rabbi's wife. This can be interpreted as a desire to serve dishes as similar as possible to those the rabbi is familiar with, hoping to create an atmosphere of friendship and closeness at the communal meal. The theme of "the king's cook who imitates the cooking of the Jewish wife" is widespread in tales dealing with Shabbat and the special taste of its characteristic dish, *cholent*.

However, at a deeper level it may have a different significance: the rabbi's wife is called upon to function in the king's private domain in the proximity of a total stranger—the male cook—without any protection. In this domain, there is a danger that the rabbi's wife will be taken away by another man of greater authority and power than his own. Similarly, the desire to cook a dish that is similar to the stew cooked by the woman for her husband can be interpreted as the desire to acquire the intimacy existing between husband and wife—her acts of giving and concern for her husband. The audience, aware of the king's intentions, feels the dissonance between his intention and the manner in which the other characters interpret his actions. They may understand the complexity of the situation and project from it to their own existence. The implicit message is clear: one must be careful and not trust anyone; one must suspect the intentions of the other even when the other is kind and welcoming.

The food described in the tale is couscous. The narrator describes the way to cook couscous and its main ingredients: bits of dough, vegetables, and meat, which are all cooked separately. In other couscous recipes, the vegetables and meat are cooked together as a soup, the dough bits are placed over it in a colander, and the flavors are absorbed from the steaming soup.[1] This dish was common in all parts of North Africa among Jews and non-Jews alike, but the narrator nevertheless appropriates it to his own community: "a special Moroccan dish made of dough bits with vegetables and meat," and feels the need to describe it.[2] Nowadays, couscous is well known both in Israel and throughout the Jewish world and is one component of Israeli cuisine.[3] However, when the tale was recorded, in 1963, it is

1 See, for example, couscous recipes: Levy-Mellul 1982: 18–26; Rodin 1980: 201–3.
2 On the origin and distribution of couscous throughout North Africa and Sicily, see Marks 2010:146–47.
3 On the status of couscous among French Jews, see Roden 1999a: 419–20.

possible that members of the Moroccan community thought that in Israel people were not familiar with their kitchen.

Later in the story, once the food had been prepared, the king and the rabbi sit down to dine. At this point, everything still seems to be all right. The rabbi's wife serves the plate to her husband. But then, just before eating, the king demands from the rabbi a surprising and inexplicable request; to remove his cloak—an act that can be symbolically interpreted as removing the rabbi from his respectable identity, and also conveys disrespect in exposing him undressed to public eyes. The rabbi carries out the request, but a certain reservation is insinuated when the narrator chooses the expression "accepted the decree." This can hint at the change in trust the rabbi has in the king. Now the deception is revealed to the audience. The king switches the kosher and nonkosher couscous the rabbi's wife and his cook prepared, respectively. Despite the almost complete likeness of the plates, the Jewish rabbi does not fall into the trap. He insists on keeping his tradition and is careful not to eat the food he was not watching, thus restoring his lost honor. The rabbi describes his custom as a family tradition, but it is possible to find some foundation for it in written sources, for example: "He 'should look at it', so as not to divert his attention from it. For this reason, there is an authority who disqualifies a narrow-mouthed cup (called a *clug glass*) from being used for Grace, because one cannot see the wine inside it. This is incorrect, for one is not required to look at the wine, but rather at the cup, so that he will not divert his attention from it" (Shulḥan Arukh, Orach Chaim, Laws of Birkat Hamazon 183:9).

The king is deeply impressed by the rabbi's wisdom, and thanks to it, by Judaism as well, and chooses to convert not only himself but all his subjects too. In this tale, group identity is saved by preserving the principle of eating kosher.

R. Israel Avidani in the Ishmaelite Town

IFA 13362

Told and Recorded by
Aluan Avidani, Kurdistan Iraq

This happened to my uncle, whose name was Israel Avidani, may his soul rest in peace.

Once he went to a town, all of its residents Ishmaelites, and stayed there for a few days.[1] He was forced to eat food from the local home-owners and break the Jewish rules just in order to survive.

A landlady brought him a very nice pita bread warm from the oven. And she brought him goat butter and yogurt. And he ate until satisfied.

Then the landlady came and said to him: "Jew, eat more, more of that. For today the bread is very tasty, because today I had water from a fresh meat stock, and I used it in the dough. That's why it tastes very good. Please eat more."

When he heard this, there was hardly any spirit and soul left in him, and he passed out.

He immediately left and went home and fasted a few fasts and in public he yelled and said, "People, this is what happened to me. Therefore, do not call me anymore by the name of Israel, but rather call me 'The one who ate despised food, meat with milk, gentiles' dishes'."

He was sorry and regretted it until his last day.

---

1 The reference is to Muslims.

Discussion of
"R. Israel Avidani in the Ishmaelite Town"

The storyteller, Aluan Avidani, was born in 1888 in Amadya, in the northern part of Kurdistan, situated at 37°05′33″N, 43°29′14″E. He immigrated to Israel in 1934. Ninety-two of his tales are registered at IFA. This one was filed in the archives in 1981.

This tale deals with the dangerous situation where Jews eat gentiles' food. It describes an extreme event: a starving man who in order to survive is coerced into eating essential food prepared by a non-Jew. Even in this case, when eating is supposedly necessary, the conclusion of the tale is that there is no choice but to maintain boundaries, and one must refrain from eating gentiles' food as ordered by Jewish law and described in the Mishnah:

> These are the things of gentiles that are forbidden but it is not forbidden to derive any benefit from them: Milk that was milked without a Jew watching, their (gentiles') bread, their oil (Rabbi and his court permitted their oil), stewed and pickled vegetables in which it is a custom (for gentiles) to put wine and vinegar, and their minced (literally, mixed) fish (literally, sardines), brine that does not have fish floating in it, chileq fish, a leaf of asafoetida, and sal-conditum. These are the things of gentiles that are forbidden but it is not forbidden to derive any benefit from them. (Mishnah Avoda Zarah 2:6)

The food described in the tale is inviting and delicious: freshly baked bread and fresh dairy products served by an Ishmaelite landlady, a kind of seductive woman. Already in rabbinical literature, this concern is mentioned: Gentile women would seduce Jewish men and convert them to idolatry using a soft approach, like offering them nonkosher refreshments.[1] Despite the innocent appearance of the bread, it was prepared in a way that completely contradicts the laws of kashrut: using water where meat not properly slaughtered was blanched, served with butter and yogurt (thus mixing meat and milk), and baked in nonkosher utensils and oven.

At first glance it seems that the Jew had no other choice but to eat in order to save his life. Therefore his actions were justified. At a deeper level, however, some criticism emerges concerning the Jew's behavior. There is no explanation for the circumstances that led the protagonist to leave home, to visit a non-Jewish space, and to remain there for a few days until he had to eat there. This issue remains obscure even to the end of the story. After the incident, the Jew returned home immediately, so it is not clear why he did not do so earlier when he was starving. While he is in the space of the "other," who is referred to in symbolic language as "a city full of Ishmaelites," he is portrayed as passive—he does not investigate the origin of the food and its method of cooking, behaving like a child who receives his food from a female figure. In the end, without him making any inquiry about the cooking, the landlady is the one who provides the Jew with information on how the bread was prepared. Only then does his behavior change. He becomes active and hurries home. Symbolically, the meaning of returning home is a return to "our space," which is secure, strengthening his identity and protecting him from violations due to getting too close to the "other." This return is also an internal process, accompanied by great sorrow and an attempt to atone for his sin. He does this in three ways. First, by fasting, an act opposite to eating. Second, by publicly confessing the sin that he committed. In other words, he performs a kind of atonement—a social act—after he had crossed the lines that define Jewish group identity—in this case maintaining kashrut. And third, by changing his identity, deleting his name and adopting a nickname based on his

---

1 See, for example, Jerusalem Talmud Sanhedrin, chapter 10, f28, 4b.

offenses—a permanent statement that removes him from "our space" and places him on its margins.

This tale has an affinity with the personal narratives' genre, as the protagonist shares family ties with the narrator. He committed infractions of the Torah's restrictions, and telling his fate constitutes a warning against contact with non-Jewish society. By describing his agony, actions, and desire to atone for the transgression, his image improves. His great sorrow and atonement can play a role in creating social cohesion and in strengthening the sacred norm of kashrut observance.

There Is No Trust in a Gentile Even after Forty Years

IFA 3060

Told by Flora Cohen, Egypt
Recorded by Ilana Zohar

A Jewish rabbi employed a non-Jewish cook in his house, who for forty years prepared all his meals according to all Jewish dietary laws.

One day the stew spoiled and it was already time to eat. What did the gentile do? He went and cooked a rabbit, which is quick and easy to cook but is forbidden to eat.

When the rabbi ate the rabbit, he suddenly saw a toe from its leg and realized that it was not a rooster. He immediately called the cook and asked him to explain it to him. At first, the cook stammered and said it was a hen and not any other animal. But in the end, he admitted to the act and asked the rabbi's forgiveness, saying that he would not repeat it.

The rabbi shook his head and said: "From this moment on you are fired from your job, because I have discovered that there is no faith in the gentile even after forty years of living together."

Discussion of
"There Is No Trust in a Gentile
Even after Forty Years"

The storyteller, Flora Cohen, was born in 1921 in Cairo, Egypt. She immigrated to Israel in 1948. Most of her tales she heard from her father in her young childhood. Eighty-four of them are registered in her name at IFA, all recorded by her daughter, Ilana Zohar. This tale was filed in the archives in 1960.

This tale is woven around a very common proverb, "Do not trust a gentile even after forty years," that appears in many Jewish folktales.[1] The common issue in all of them is the constant failure of Jews who attempt to put their trust in gentiles. This tale describes two characters, a Jewish rabbi and his gentile cook, who collaborated for forty years, until finally the relationship of trust between them was undermined by the gentile's actions.

The issue is presented in a very subtle manner because at the plot's center stands a rabbi, a figure whose main responsibility is the observance of Jewish law, but who chose to entrust the cooking to a gentile. Kashrut forms a central part of Jewish law. Keeping a kosher home ensures that this is a space that allows a Jew to preserve his identity. This space is maintained when the cook, who is in charge of the kitchen, keeps kosher himself, and in order to ensure this, he must belong to the group. Therefore, when the cook does not "belong" because he is a gentile, one can reasonably assume

---

1 A detailed discussion of this proverb can be found in Hasan-Rokem 1978, 63–80. The tale before us is presented in an appendix (p. 251), along with twelve additional IFA tales in which this proverb is included. There are in IFA's collection twenty-four tales belonging to the oicotype: AT 910*M, Do Not Believe a Gentile, Even Forty Years after His Death.

that problems will arise. Any practicing Jew faces this issue. Ferris Cohen has studied this problem among American homemakers (Cohen Ferris 2015, 141).

Common Jewish directives forbid eating foods cooked by a gentile, if not attended by a Jew. For example: "A food that is not eaten when it is raw and is served at a kings table, to spread on bread or as a dessert, which was cooked by a non-Jew, even in the pots of Jews and in the house of a Jew, it is forbidden because it was cooked by a non-Jew" (Shulḥan Arukh Yoreh Deah 113, a).

This is eventually the case described in the tale. For an unexplained reason, cooking in the rabbi's house is the responsibility of a non-Jewish cook, an ominous fact that he finally realizes is a mistake. For forty years, the cook performed his work faithfully and maintained a kosher kitchen, but despite the long time that elapsed and despite the cook's great experience, when a problem arises and he is unable to serve kosher food, he cooks a nonkosher animal. The rabbit is forbidden to eat according to explicit statements in the Torah: "Nevertheless these shall ye not eat of them that chew the cud, or of them that divide the hoof. . . . And the hare, because he cheweth the cud, but divideth not the hoof; he is unclean unto you" (Leviticus 11:4–6). And in another almost identical phrasing: "Nevertheless these ye shall not eat of them that chew the cud, or of them that divide the cloven hoof; as the camel, and the hare, and the coney: for they chew the cud, but divide not the hoof; therefore they are unclean unto you" (Deuteronomy 14:7).

Since it is clear that this is not an error stemming from the cook's lack of knowledge, he is fired. The correctness of the proverb is proved once again. On a deeper level there is a criticism of the rabbi, who relied on an outsider to deal with a sensitive issue that concerns Jewish daily life. This criticism is reinforced by the proverb, which expresses collective wisdom that stands the test of time.

BATEL BASHISHIM—
ONE-SIXTIETH IS NEGLIGIBLE

IFA 9782

TOLD BY RAPHAEL COHEN, LITHUANIA
RECORDED BY MALKA COHEN

In a small town in Lithuania, a poor Jew came to the rabbi and in tears told him that in the pot he cooked a soup in fell a small piece of pork. What will he eat from now on, has all his food become unfit to eat?

The rabbi took pity on the poor Jew and asked him, "What was the amount of soup and what size was the piece of pork that fell into the soup?"

The Jew told him how big it was. The rabbi calculated and told him that the pork was one-sixtieth of the soup and therefore *batel bashishim*—the amount was negligible and he was allowed to eat the soup.

Later the rabbi met the same Jew and saw that his face had improved. The rabbi asked him why.

The Jew said: "Rabbi, every day I put in my soup pot a piece of *batel bashishim* and it adds to my health."

Discussion of
"*Batel Bashishim*—
One-Sixtieth Is Negligible"

The storyteller, Raphael Cohen, was born in Siubaiciai (Shubots, in Yiddish), situated in northern Lithuania, 55°55″ N, 23°30″ E. He immigrated to Israel in 1921. At IFA nine tales are registered in his name. His wife, Malka Cohen, recorded all of them. This tale was filed in the archives in 1973.

This is a short anecdote that presents an absurd situation resulting from a permissive interpretation of the laws of kashrut. The use of humor enables discussion of the complex issue of a lenient approach to the law and the danger thereof.

The ruling standing at the plot's center is called *batel bashishim*: one-sixtieth is negligible. Its meaning is that if kosher food gets mixed with nonkosher food, in some cases the mixture may be eaten if the amount of kosher food is at least sixty times greater than the quantity of nonkosher food. For example:

"If a drop of milk fell onto a piece of meat and it imparted some flavor unto that piece, it is forbidden. If the pot was stirred, then it [the entire pot] is forbidden only if [the drop of milk] imparted some flavor into [all that was in] the pot." Raba said: In the past the following was always a difficulty to me. It was taught: In a pot wherein meat had been cooked a person may not boil milk, and if he did boil [milk] therein, it depends whether the pot imparted a flavour [to the milk] or not. (Mishnah Hullin 8:3)

And also:

Raba also said, [In certain cases] the Rabbis ruled that the test whether or not it imparts a flavour applies, and [in other cases] the Rabbis ruled that one may rely upon a [Gentile] cook, and yet [in other cases] the Rabbis ruled that the test is sixty [to one]. Therefore we say, where substances of different kinds, each kind being permitted by itself, were mixed together, the test is whether or not one imparts a flavour to the other; and if one of the substances was forbidden, then we rely upon the opinion of a Gentile cook. Where substances of like kind were mixed together, in which case it is impossible to discern whether one imparts a flavour to the other; or where substances of different kinds, one of which was forbidden, were mixed together, and no [Gentile] cook is available, then the test is sixty [to one]. (Babylonian Talmud Hullin 97a–b)

Relying on this ruling, the rabbi in the tale allows the poor man to eat from the dish. The latter exploits the permit, out of either ignorance or foolishness, and deliberately continues to mix his cooked dishes with pieces of pork equivalent to one-sixtieth according to *batel bashishim*.

Two strata can be discerned in the tale: On its face, at the beginning of the tale the poor man is in a dire state, and after his encounter with the rabbi his situation improves; he is no longer gaunt and hungry, but satiated and healthy. The audience listening to the tale is clearly aware that the solution the poor man found is inappropriate and that he is abusing the rabbi's ruling.

The rabbi's ruling may be understood not only as stemming from Jewish dietary law but from other sources as well. One is the empathy he feels toward the poor of his community, and his recognition of the harsh reality they face: their difficulty in obtaining food and the hunger that frequently afflicts them. Another is a prudent concern to prevent the wasting of expensive products that are hard to obtain, namely the soup mixed with pork, liable to be thrown away for not being kosher. The rabbi must navigate between the obligation to observe the laws of kashrut and the desire to ease the economic distress of the members of his community.

At a deeper level, the question arises: Does adherence to the laws of kashrut worsen the poor man's condition, or at least keep him in his miserable state? The audience may wonder whether, even though the poor man's solution is wrong, it has merit for allowing him to overcome the distress caused by strict adherence to the law. Or was the ruling in this case too lenient, allowing it to be interpreted incorrectly? Ultimately it seems like this quandary is resolved by the mere fact that the case involves pork specifically. The prohibition against eating pork is not a postbiblical accretion but directly from the Torah (Leviticus 11:7, Deuteronomy 14:8), where the pig is mentioned among the other forbidden animals. And in postbiblical tradition, pork comes to symbolize the food of the "other." In Jewish collective memory, it was consumed by people who persecuted the Jews and forced them to eat its meat. The pig became a symbol of an abomination that Jews were so unwilling to eat that they preferred dying as martyrs than to eat it. An example is the story of Eliezer the elder, who chose just that: to die rather than eat pork as ordered by the Romans (2 Maccabees 6:21–38).

Although some humorous tales deal with the amusing attempt to "legalize" pork by kosher slaughter and salting its meat, it is clear that they reinforce the conclusion that it is impossible.[1] Even if in our tale the rabbi, as the representative of Jewish law, "koshers" the soup, in folk consciousness this is an unacceptable act. The restrictions in folk consciousness may be even stricter than those of the established laws of kashrut, from fear, actually verified in this tale, that breaching the borders will eventually lead to a blurring of Jewish identity. This identity is symbolized by a strict abstention from pork.

---

1 For example, the tale "How to Slaughter a Pig in a Kosher Way" (IFA 14799). Narratives about turning pork into kosher meat can be found among Jews of the former Soviet Union: see Jochnowitz 2011, 377.

The Butter Cake
of Pasha-Leah

IFA 10660

Told by Hannah Shneid, Poland
Recorded by Avraham Keren

On the eve of Shavuot, Pasha-Leah prepares for the holiday. She cooks and bakes for the Shavuot holiday a usual butter cake and a dish of meat. She is also busy with other preparations for the holiday. Suddenly she hears that something has boiled over in the kitchen. She runs in to see what happened. And there, Oh no! the meat soup boiled over and spilled on the butter cake. Nothing can be done, the cake is now unfit to be consumed.

Still, she thought, I will go and ask the rabbi. She runs to the rabbi and asks her question: "Here, the soup spilled over the holiday's butter cake. Is the cake kosher or unfit to eat?" She asks anxiously and hesitantly.

The rabbi hears her story and rules: "The cake is kosher."

Pasha-Leah does not believe her ears, and without realizing it, she says to herself: Is it possible? A butter cake with meat soup is a kosher cake?

The rabbi answers her again: "Yes, Leah, the cake is kosher." And she stands wondering and still hesitates. The rabbi sees her hesitation and calms her: "Rest your mind, I'm sure that Pasha-Leah's butter cake has flour, water, and more, but there is certainly no butter."

Discussion of
"THE BUTTER CAKE OF PASHA-LEAH"

The storyteller, Hannah Shneid, was born in Lviv, situated in western Ukraine: 49°49′48″N, 24°00′51″E. No further biographical information is provided in the archives. Five tales are registered in her name at IFA. This tale was filed in 1974.

The halakhic background to the tale is an issue called in Jewish law "meat in milk" which refers to the Torah prohibition of cooking a goat kid in its mother's milk: "Thou shalt not seethe a kid in his mother's milk," a decree that is repeated three times in the Torah (Exodus 23:19, Exodus 34:26, Deuteronomy 14:21).

This dictate was developed and expanded in Rabbinic laws to prohibit the cooking, eating, and serving of any meat with milk and dairy products. For example: "All types of meat are forbidden to be cooked in milk, except for the flesh of fish and of locusts; and it is forbidden to place upon the table [any meat] with cheese, except for fish and the meat of locusts" (Mishnah Hullin 8:1).[1]

The time frame mentioned in the plot is the eve of the festival of Shavuot.[2] The foods typical of this festival are dairy and meat, represented in this tale by a butter cake and meat soup.[3] This Eastern European custom is derived from a fifteenth century source: "During Shavuot, we eat milk

---

1 See also Babylonian Talmud Hullin 104a–113a; Shulḥan Arukh Yoreh Deah 87:4.

2 The topic of eating during the holidays is discussed at length in the next chapter.

3 For a recipe of butter cake containing flour, sugar, egg, butter, and a pinch of salt, that is, the ingredients that are likely almost identical to those in our tale, see Roden 1999a, 167.

remembering what is hinted in the Torah (Numbers 28:26) in the acronym MHLV [Hebrew *mehalav*, 'from milk']. And meat must be eaten as well, because there is no joy without meat" (Tyrnau 1884, 13).[4]

The woman at the center of the plot has a very important role in transitioning from secular to sacred time: she must prepare and cook delicacies worthy of the holiday. These foods require more effort than usual, because the investment in transforming the food from its natural state to a cultural status is considerable. According to Lévi-Strauss's models, nature is considered lesser and opposed to culture, which is the highest level of refinement. Therefore, the farther food is removed from its natural state, and the longer it is processed and cooked, the more it improves, getting closer to a "culture" state befitting human—and holiday—consumption (Lévi-Strauss 1969). The woman must effectively manage the limited time she has to enter the sacred time when its culinary symbols, the holiday foods, are ready.

In addition, as a Jewish woman who observes kashrut, she must strictly separate meat from milk.[5] The drama takes place when the meat soup is accidentally poured over the butter cake. According to the woman, the cake has become unkosher and can no longer be eaten. Still, perhaps because she is so desperate to avoid discarding the cake, the woman turns to the rabbi. Her petition is described as hesitant since she speculates on the answer— she interprets the incident as a strict and convincing case that the cake is invalid. To her great surprise, and to the audience's surprise, the rabbi determines that the butter cake is kosher. The doubt expressed by the woman toward the rabbi's answer is also an expression of the doubts of the audience.

The rabbi's surprising explanation—that the cake does not contain butter—is not based on information previously provided in the tale. We do not know why the cake does not contain butter. A possible explanation

---

4   For additional sources and halakhic issues that stem from eating meat and milk on Shavuot, see Farkash 1996.

5   On the centrality of women in strict observance of a kosher kitchen, as "sanctifiers of the profane," see Sered 1992, 88–90 and Myerhoff 1978, 210.

is that the cook is a stingy woman who does not want to add butter to the cake. But there is no hint in the story itself that indicates this. Another possibility, perhaps more likely, is that due to the financial distress of the protagonist, she cannot get butter. A very considerate rabbi is depicted here. He does not mention her economic situation but knows it well, and his ruling prevents further distress and the loss of expensive food.

Here lies the unexpected sting in the tale: In order to understand the rabbi's statement, the audience must complete the vital information lacking in the tale that supports his rulings, namely the cook's poverty. The surprise of hiding this vital information is humorous.[6] Paradoxically, poverty turns from being a burden to a solution, because it ensures the maintenance of kosher food, although most kashrut laws burden the poor. At the end of the tale, we can breathe a sigh of relief. In the protagonist's home, in honoring the holiday all the delicacies prepared will be present on the table.

---

6 According to the models of David Navon (1981, 144).

5

FISH IN HONOR

OF THE SHABBAT

FOOD AND SACRED TIME

F ood is one of the means by which one distinguishes between secular time and sacred time. These terms were coined by Mircea Eliade, who sought to characterize types existing in traditional societies (1965). According to Eliade's definitions, secular time is the daily time. It begins at a certain point and proceeds linearly. Each passing moment differs from the past one or the one to come. As the pre-Socratic philosopher Heraclitus put it, "*Panta rhei*"—everything flows.

Differing from secular time, sacred time—the time of holidays and festivals—is recurring and cyclical. During the sacred time, foundational events, such as the creation of the world and the creation of the nation, are perpetuated and eternalized through commemoration. These events are depicted through myths.

Often sacred time sees changes in eating habits and the types of foods consumed.[1] Some sacred times are characterized by abstinence from eating (Bynum 1987). Transitioning from secular time to sacred time and living in

---

1 For example, see a description of ritual eating among the Arunta tribe in Australia: Durkheim 1971, 326–36.

sacred time are accompanied by rituals.[2] These consist of symbols that facilitate an understanding of the ritual and its goals. These symbols are tangible and act by evoking strong emotions, both consciously and unconsciously, through all the human senses. Food naturally activates all the senses and is, in many cases, incorporated as symbols in these rituals. By studying these symbols, one becomes acquainted with a society's system of values and norms (Turner 1967).

Jewish sacred time, also called by some researchers *qualitative time* (Bar-Itzhak 1987), involves periodic changes in nature, such as changes of the seasons and agricultural phases. For example, three festivals—Pesach, Shavuot, and Sukkot—have an immanent connection to the cycle of the agricultural year: the ripening of grain, the appearance of the first fruits, and the end of harvest, respectively. It also involves historical events, such as the Exodus from Egypt and the giving of the Torah (Gaster 1961). Holidays and festivals are the memory and the commemoration of constitutive events in the history of the nation (Hevlin 2009). Foods that characterize Jewish sacred time are not only signs of holiness, but also memorializing symbols.[3] As such, they connect people to the overall value system of their society and thereby strengthen cultural identity.

Jewish sacred time periods are characterized by festive meals designed to distinguish them from secular time. With this purpose, these meals are composed of exquisite and expensive dishes usually absent from the dining table of everyday life (Jochnowitz 2013; Kirshenblatt-Gimblett 2010). Often preparation of these foods requires skill and time (Bahloul 1983), which further distinguishes them as appropriate to sacred time.

---

2 There are different definitions of the term *ritual*. Some scholars have sorted rituals by types. See, for example, a distinction between six types (Grimes 1995, 40–57). The definition used in this discussion is, "The performance of more or less invariant sequences of formal acts and utterances not entirely encoded by the performers" (Rappaport 2002, 24).

3 On the connection between food and memory, see Holtzman 2006; Horowitz 2014.

In addition, each holiday is characterized by certain foods, a distinguishing mark sometimes referred to as "holiday signs." For example, the Talmud recommends various dishes for a Rosh Hashanah (New Year) meal: "Said Abaye: Now that it has been said that omens are of significance, a man should make a regular habit of eating, at the beginning of the year, pumpkin, fenugreek, leek, beet and dates" (Babylonian Talmud, Horayot 12a; Kritot 6a). These specific foods act as carriers of identity and memory. The clearest example is, of course, the matzah, the "bread of affliction" eaten on Passover, which symbolizes the historical chapter of Israel's slavery in the land of Egypt: "Thou shalt eat no leavened bread with it; seven days shalt thou eat unleavened bread therewith, even the bread of affliction; for thou camest forth out of the land of Egypt in haste: that thou mayest remember the day when thou camest forth out of the land of Egypt all the days of thy life" (Deuteronomy 16:3).

Traditional dishes specifically prepared for Jewish sacred times have two main sources. One is established religion: Torah decrees and their later interpretations, such as for the Passover eve meal—the seder. The Torah mentions three components of the meal that are eaten to this day on seder night as well as throughout the holiday: meat, matzah (unleavened bread), and maror (bitter herbs): "And they shall eat the flesh in that night, roast with fire, and unleavened bread; and with bitter herbs they shall eat it" (Exodus 12:8). The prohibition of eating leavened bread—*hametz*—during the seven days of Passover is given in the Torah: "Seven days shall ye eat unleavened bread; even the first day ye shall put away leaven out of your houses: for whosoever eateth leavened bread from the first day until the seventh day, that soul shall be cut off from Israel" (Exodus 12:15). Additional dishes of the Seder meal that are customary today are based on a Rabbinical description (Mishnah Pesachim 10:1–8).

The other source for the traditional dishes of Jewish sacred time is folklore, which occasionally discovers associative and interpretive connections that make particular foods apt for particular occasions. Some traditions were borrowed from non-Jewish cultures, amongst whom various Jewish communities lived, such as challah, which originated from German braided bread used in pagan ritual (Ben-Yossef 2006) or hamantashen, a common Eastern European pastry whose name in Yiddish, *mohntashen* (poppy seed pockets), was reminiscent of *Haman*, the name of the evil protagonist in the Purim festival.

One of the most sacred times in the Jewish calendar is Shabbat. Due to its constant weekly occurrences, it is the most representative of Jewish sacred time and has all its characteristics. For example, a Midrash describes the practical means to experience the holiness of Shabbat:

> It is said (Exodus 20:8): "Remember the Shabbat day, to keep it holy," How can you sanctify it? What is it that you sanctify? With food and drinks, and clean garments. Your Shabbat meal should not be like your daily meal, and your Shabbat garments not like your daily ones. And from where do we learn it? That even a poor person should not eat on Shabbat the same food he eats during the week. And the rich shall not eat on Shabbat the food of the mundane. We learn it from: "Remember the Shabbat day, to keep it holy." (Mekhilta of Rabbi Shimon bar Yochai, 20)

On Shabbat, unique dishes are served surpassing in quality and cost the daily dishes eaten during the rest of the week. The Torah does not directly mention the foods that should be eaten on Shabbat, but there is an explicit prohibition against lighting fire during Shabbat: "Ye shall kindle no fire throughout your habitations upon the Shabbat day" (Exodus 35:3). The desire to celebrate Shabbat with special foods while adhering to the prohibition of cooking that day required creative culinary solutions. Among certain ethnic groups (Ethiopians, Samaritans, Karaites) the answer is to eat cold food. However, in most communities, the solution is to serve *hamin*, a hot meat stew (today there are also vegetarian versions) prepared before Shabbat and baked for hours in a heated oven, lit before but not during Shabbat. Different ethnic groups have their own versions, ingredients, and appellations for this dish: *cholent* or *tsholnt* in Eastern Europe, *shena* or *dafina* in North Africa (on the *dafina* as an archetypal food, see Bahloul 1983, 221), *harisa* in Tunisia, *osh-sobo* in Bukhara, *tabit* in Iraq, and *shfta* in Kurdistan.

Originally, the term *hamin* was used in Rabbinical literature for "hot water" (e.g., Babylonian Talmud Shabbat 22b). The same term, but in the sense of a special dish for Shabbat, appears in the twelfth century in the writings of R. Zechariah Halevy Grondy (1125–86) in the context of a dispute with the Karaites over whether it is permitted to continue cooking during the Shabbat: "Our sages ruled that Shabbat delight is in the *hamin*. Anyone who does not eat *hamin* has to be checked if he is not a heretic" (Klein 2006).

The term *cholent* is also mentioned around the same time (1180) by R. Yitzhak ben Moshe of Vienna: "I saw in France in the home of my teacher R. Yehuda bar Yitzhak that sometimes their cholent pots were buried. And on Shabbat before the meal, the servants light the fire near the cauldrons so that they warm well and some remove them and bring them close to the fire" (Or Zaruah, part 2, Hilhot Erev Shabbat, 3b).

The origin of some traditional Shabbat dishes stemmed indirectly from descriptions found in the Torah, such as the double portion of manna the Israelites collected on Friday and was sufficient for eating also on Shabbat (Exodus 16:4–5). This event has been linked to several customs: one is placing two loaves of bread on the dinner table at the Kabbalat Shabbat—the ceremony marking the beginning of Shabbat—based on a Rabbinical interpretation: "Rabbi Abba said: On Shabbat one should break bread from two loaves. What is the reason? As it is written (Exodus 16:22): 'And it came to pass, that on the sixth day they gathered twice as much bread, two omers for one man: and all the rulers of the congregation came and told Moses'" (Babylonian Talmud Berachot 39b).

Another custom connected to this event is to obtain in advance food products required for the Shabbat meals. Some commentaries explain this custom by pointing to a biblical source. For example, in the Talmud: "R. Hisda said: One should always make early preparations against the termination of the Shabbat, for it is said (Exodus 16:5) 'And it shall come to pass on the sixth day, that they shall prepare that which they bring in immediately'" (Babylonian Talmud Shabbat 117b). From a medieval source: "Even a very important person who is unaccustomed to buying items at the marketplace or to doing housework is required to perform tasks to prepare by himself for the Shabbat. This is an expression of his own personal honor" (Maimonides, *Mishneh Torah*, Shabbat, 30:6). In the halakhah (the religious law): "One should always wake up on Friday mornings to prepare for Shabbat, for Moses warned us at the descent of the manna" (Exodus 16:5), "they shall prepare that which they bring in" (Yihiel Michal Halevi Epshtein, *Aruch Hashulhan*, Orach Haim, Preparing Shabbat Meal, 250 A).

An additional custom is to eat three meals during Shabbat. This is also based on a Rabbinical interpretation: "Our Rabbis taught: How many meals must one eat on the Shabbat? Three. R. Hidka said: Four. R. Johanan observed, both expound the same verse" (Exodus 16:25): "And Moses said, Eat that today; for today is a Shabbat unto the Lord: today ye shall not find it in the field" (Babylonian Talmud, Shabbat 117b).

Another tradition is based on the connection between Shabbat and pleasure. This pleasure is called *Oneg Shabbat* (Shabbat delight), according to Isaiah 58:13: "And you shall call the Shabbat a delight." One of its concrete expressions is eating distinctive dishes reserved only for Shabbat. Some of the dishes are described as early as the Talmud. For example:

Rab Judah said in Rab's name: He who delights in the Shabbat is granted his heart's desires, for it is said (Psalms 37:4): "Delight thyself also in the Lord; And he shall give thee the desires of thine heart." Now, I do not know what this "delight" refers to; but when it is said: "And thou shalt call the Shabbat a delight" you must say that it refers to the delight of the Shabbat. Wherewith does one show his delight therein?—Rab Judah son of R. Samuel b. Shilath said in Rab's name: With a dish of beets, large fish, and heads of garlic. R. Hiyya b. Ashi said in Rab's name: Even a trifle, if it is prepared in honor of the Shabbat, is delight. What is it [the trifle]?—Said R. Papa: A pie of fish-hash. (Babylonian Talmud Shabbat 118b)

Folktales dealing with the foods of Jewish sacred time vary in their content. Some deal with sensitive issues, a major one being the economic burden of obtaining and preparing food for the sacred time, especially on Passover and on Shabbat. On Passover, the economic burden is expressed in the procurement of wine, matzah, and kosher meat proper for the holiday. For example, one tale focuses on doubt about a turkey bought for Passover, in whose stomach a grain of wheat was found. Wheat being a forbidden food on Passover, does it affect the whole fowl?[4] Ingredients that are the most challenging to obtain for the Shabbat dinner due to their relatively high cost, and of course kashrut issues, are wine, meat, and fish.

A famous talmudic story tells of the pauper R. Hanina ben Dosa and his wife who were unable to buy any food for the Shabbat (Babylonian Talmud Taanit 24b–25a). In despair, the poor wife lights the empty stove. Eventually the food is provided miraculously by some mysterious stranger. This story is prevalent nowadays. In some versions, the protagonists are anonymous, a detail that can point to economic distress that became widespread across the communities telling this tale.[5]

Another issue raised in folktales is the link between holiness and food, as a cause and effect. Two questions are examined: One is whether food can generate the feeling of sacred time. This question is raised, for example, in the Hasidic tale "Feeling the Shabbat" (Buber 1965, 224), in which two brothers, Rabbi Elimelech and Rabbi Zusia, seek to ascertain whether the sense of holiness surrounding them on Shabbat is true or dependent on their special behavior on this day.

---

4 The tale is "Three Reasons to make life easier" (IFA 13749), already mentioned in the introduction to the second chapter of this book.

5 For an additional explanation of the anonymity of the figures of the sages in IFA's versions of the Rabbinical tales, see Stein 2016.

The second question is whether sacred time has special attributes that influence the taste of food. An ancient and well-known midrash tackling this question is known by the title "The Taste of Shabbat," in which Antoninus, the Roman leader, is invited to eat both on Shabbat and during the week and wonders about the different taste of the food. "Our Teacher made a meal for Antoninus on Shabbat. Cold dishes were set before him; he ate them and found them delicious. On another occasion he made a meal for him during the week, when hot dishes were set before him. He said to him: 'Those others I enjoyed more'. 'These lack a certain condiment', he replied. 'Does then the royal pantry lack anything?' he exclaimed. 'They lack the Shabbat', he retorted, 'do you indeed possess the Shabbat?'" (Bereshit Rabba 11:4).

Some folktales are of an etiological nature, providing explanations for the origin of the eating customs observed during sacred times. Certain researchers (e.g., Gaster 1961) have suggested that holidays are an expression and response to an event in nature, a "crisis," in their terminology. At the time of Passover, for example, a transition from winter to spring is occurring, a sort of awakening and resurrection after the hibernation or death of nature. The holiday aims to facilitate this passage. It also celebrates the birth of the Jewish people. It faces down the fear that death may return in the form of threats to the life of the community such as blood libels. Indeed, numerous folktales reflect the assumption that sacred time constitutes a period of crisis, especially Passover, and indeed link sacred time to the historical reality of blood libels against the Jews.

Other tales use humor to transmit self-criticism—for example, the Jewish people's failure to fast when called for. Such is the tale "Odd People": "One day a week, they eat in the dining room and smoke in the bathroom (on Shabbat). One day a year, they smoke in the dining room but eat in the bathroom (on the 9th of Av). Another day a year they eat and also smoke in the bathroom (on Yom Kippur). Odd people!" (IFA 15742). Some tales ridicule the dishes of sacred time, such as *cholent*, which may cause digestive troubles. For example, two tales from IFA's collection describe as a miracle the fact that Jews are still alive after eating it: "I Believe in Resurrection" (IFA 5741) and "Resurrection" (IFA 15658).

There are other tales that deal with Jewish identity and its affinity to the foods of sacred time. Such tales are about converts from Judaism who, on smelling or tasting Shabbat *cholent*, become nostalgic for the religion they have abandoned or are even induced to return to Judaism. This topic is broached in the second tale of this chapter.

This chapter contains five tales dealing with the links between eating customs and the sacred time of Shabbat, Passover, and Shavuot. They touch on the expression of Jewish identity through these customs. Two of them even present amusing etiological explanations for the link between food and sacred time.

R. Eliyahu Buhbut and the Fish on Shabbat Eve

IFA 6437

Told by Yosef Mashash, Morocco
Recorded by Moshe Rabi

Rabbi Eliyahu Buhbut when he arrived in Meknes stayed with the rich man Shlomo Boyder. In Morocco, the Jews used to eat fish on Shabbat eve. Friday came, and it happened that no fish were to be found in the market. Shlomo Boyder sent his servant to look for fish and bring them at any price. The servant wandered around all the markets and all the fish shops, and could not find even one fish. The rich man Shlomo Boyder was deeply saddened; a distinguished guest sits in his house, and he has no fish for Shabbat; how is it possible?

Rabbi Eliyahu noticed his host was sad and asked him for the reason of his sadness.

The host said to him, "How can I not be sorry? Shabbat eve has arrived and there are no fish to honor the Shabbat."

Rabbi Eliyahu said to him, "I will get you a shad" (*alosia*), a very special fish that the Jews of Meknes are very fond of.[1] The host asked him, "From where will you bring it? There is not even one fish in the whole city."

And R. Eliyahu said to him, "I will bring you."

Shabbat eve arrived. They went together to the synagogue to welcome the Shabbat. After the prayers, they returned home. The entire house is full of light. The table is set. The members of the household are sitting at the

---

1 In his book on North African Jewish customs, Raphael Ben Simhon writes about the shad: "The Moroccan Jew as well wooed large fish for Shabbat. A special fish called *a-sabil* in Judeo-Arabic and *l'alose* in French was preferred and the tastiest" (Ben Simhon 1998, 38).

table. They sanctified the wine, said the *Hamotzi* over the bread, and all the members of the household saw a pan full of fish on the table.

The host's wife shouted, "Where is the fish from? We did not have any fish!"

R. Eliyahu answered, "These are my fish from the city of Rabat."

He reached out, took a fish from the pan, and began to eat. And the whole family ate the fish too, and it was a wonder to the whole family.

The next day, Rabbi Eliyahu received a letter from his wife, in which she complains, "You left us for a few weeks, I thought you would come back for Shabbat, I bought fish and cooked them in a frying pan, and on Friday night the pan was stolen along with the fish."

Rabbi Eliyahu showed the letter to the rich host and said to him, "Read the letter and see that we ate the same fish my wife cooked."

The host read the letter and knew that Rabbi Eliyahu was doing wonders.

Discussion of
"R. Eliyahu Buhbut and the Fish on Shabbat Eve"

T he storyteller, Rabbi Yosef Mashash, was born at the end of the nineteenth century in Meknes, in northern Morocco, situated at 33°53′42″N, 5°33′17″W. He immigrated to Israel in 1964. Thirty-eight tales are registered in his name at IFA, this one in 1965.

At the center of the tale stands a fish dish, which is presented as a sign of Shabbat among the Jews of Morocco; as it is phrased in the tale: "In Morocco the Jews used to eat fish on Friday night."[1] Fish was a prevalent dish among Moroccan Jews. Some explain it by the fact that Morocco has a long coastline, abundant with fish (Levy-Mellul 1982, 121), while others connect it to the life cycle. Fish was associated with abundance and fertility, and in Morocco, a fish meal was served to young couples a few days after their wedding (Roden 1999a, 280). Perhaps the encouragement of fertility on the night of Shabbat is actually connected to the tradition that Shabbat is a preferred time for conjugal relations.

It is reasonable to assume that this practice may have traditional Jewish sources. In Rabbinical literature, eating fish is connected to Shabbat (Toseftah Peah [Lieberman] 4:8): "For Shabbat we provide him with food for three meals: oil and beans, fish and vegetables." There, the delight of the occasion is also connected to eating fish (Babylonian Talmud

---

1 Other Jewish Moroccan folktales allude to this custom, such as "The Punishment of a Woman Who Refused to Give from the Shabbat Fish" (IFA 11546). In this tale, it is explicitly stated: "He cannot pass the Shabbat without fish"; "Your wife spoiled the Shabbat for me because of a piece of fish."

Shabbat 118b).[2] A famous ancient story also linking Shabbat to fish is called "Joseph Who Honors the Shabbat": Joseph's honor consists, in part, in buying fish weekly (Babylonian Talmud Shabbat 119a).

Our tale intertwines reality and imagination. The realistic aspect is conveyed in the identification of the two active protagonists, the host Shlomo Boyder and the guest Rabbi Eliyahu Buhbut, as well as in the place where the story takes place—Meknes and Rabat—two cities in northwestern Morocco.[3] Also realistic are the description of the *Kabbalat Shabbat* ritual, the stay in the synagogue, the blessings over the wine and the bread,[4] as well as the description of the activities connected to the fish dish: the obstinate search for fish in all the commercial areas of the city.

The inability to serve fish at the Shabbat dinner is described in the tale as a double blow, both to the honor of the guest and to the sanctity of the sacred time: "A distinguished guest sits in his house, and he has no fish for Shabbat, how is it possible? . . . How can I not be sorry? Shabbat's eve has arrived and there are no fish to honor the Shabbat."

The guest, for his part, wishes to honor his host, relieve his distress, and resolve the problem. Before the start of Shabbat, he promises his host to obtain fish. Here the two dimensions—the realistic and the supernatural—join and intertwine. In the realistic dimension, fish are not available, whereas in the supernatural dimension, a cooking pot containing the fish dish appears on the host's table. As cooked, the fish is no longer in its "savage state," but has undergone culinary processing that binds it to the cultural domain. The guest, who serves himself first, brings the plot back to the realistic dimension and emphasizes that the food is edible and not magical.

---

2 See full quotation in the introduction of this chapter.

3 Between these two cities, the distance is 150 km. The location of Meknes is 33°53′42″N, 5°33′17″W and the location of Rabat is 34°02′N, 6°50′W.

4 On the ritual of blessing over bread, see the discussion of the tale "Hosts Who Do Not Feed Their Guest" (IFA 2400), in chapter 3.

The sudden appearance of the fish dish evokes various connotations. One is related to the literary genre. The motif of obtaining food by magical means is common in folktales and characterizes fairytales.[5] A second connotation is Jesus's miracle of feeding the multitude with two small fish (Mark 6:34–44). Although the Jews in Morocco lived among Muslims, under the French Protectorate governing Morocco between 1912 and 1956, they were also likely to be exposed to French Christian culture. A third connotation relates to the Jewish motif of *kfitzat haderech*, an immediate and timeless transposition of a character, usually a person, from one place to a distant one, as described in the Babylonian Talmud (Sanhedrin 95a). Objects may also be transmitted from place to place timelessly, such as Nahmanides' ship (*Shalshelet Hakabbalah*, in Dan 1974, 159). Sometimes it occurs before Shabbat, as described in the Ahimaatz Scroll.[6]

In this tale, which is a saint's legend[7] about Rabbi Eliyahu Buhbut, the fish dish transits from place to place in honor of Shabbat. It is not an enchanted object, as is customary in the fairytale genre, but is rather an object whose sanctity derives from the miracles performed by Rabbi Eliyahu. The dish is not brought in because of gluttony, nor to solve hunger's distress, but rather to sanctify the Shabbat and to rejoice the host. Therefore, the supposedly magical action receives a moral and sacred depth and becomes a kind of miracle caused by that holy person.

In due course of the tale, which takes place mostly in the host's house in the city of Meknes, we learn about the events in the guest's home in the city of Rabat. This may be considered a reversal of the "time-leap" (since the fish came from Rabat to Meknes). The content of a letter written by Rabbi Eliyahu's wife, which the rabbi received by mail, appears to be in a realistic mode. But in terms of a realistic description of time duration, it

---

5 The motif according to Stith Thompson is D1030.1, Food Supplied by Magic (Thompson 1955, 2:128).

6 Ahimaatz Scroll, pp. 24–25, Hebrew Books, https://hebrewbooks.org/. For an extensive survey of this topic, see Verman and Adler 1993.

7 For the term and the genre definition, see Bar-Itzhak 1987.

is hardly credible: the letter was sent on Saturday night and arrived on Sunday. After the letter is read, the mystery of the source of the fish is solved: the fish was cooked by the guest's wife and miraculously transferred to the host's house. The tale concludes that this act is one of the wonders that the guest has performed.

The personal letter evokes talmudic tales about scholars studying far away during the week and who do not return to their homes for the holy days, especially the tale about Yehuda the son of R. Hiyya (Babylonian Talmud, Kethuboth 62b).

Shabbat eve is usually a time when couples have marital relations—another aspect of *Oneg Shabbat*—Shabbat delight. The complaint of Rabbi Eliyahu's wife has two elements: first she complains of the dish's theft, which has violated the sanctity of her Shabbat; indirectly we hear of the physical absence of her husband, which has lasted for several weeks. The absence of intimate relations prevents her fertility and deprives her of the opportunity to bear a child. Since fish are a symbol of fertility, the act of stealing her fish can be interpreted as the robbery of her fertility. Her complaint has an intertwined meaning, linking food and intimacy.[8] Her *Oneg Shabbat* was denied to her: she was unable to eat the sacred time's special dish and unable to engage in intimacy, rendering her, at least for a time, infertile.

The fish dish appears in the tale as a sign of the Shabbat's sanctity, but it is also interwoven in the social fabric of guest-host relations and the cohesion of Jewish communities dispersed throughout Morocco. The miraculous transfer of the dish from Rabat to Meknes symbolizes the significance of Shabbat and the preservation of this social cohesion, but also admits an affront to the Shabbat meal in the guest's own home.

---

8 See chapter 2.

The Taste of the Shabbat's *Hamin*

IFA 12396

Told by Simha Shamaka, Libya
Recorded by Rivka Peer and Penina Resnik

An egg from the *hamin* is never given to gentiles because it is said that it saves a soul. Once a Jewess wanted to convert to Islam and marry a gentile, and she did.

On Saturday, she smelled the *hamin* of the Jews and sighed. From each sigh, her husband was frightened and asked what to do for her. She remembered the egg of the hamin.

He said: "Is that what you are lacking? You can prepare a *hamin* and put eggs in it."

She did, but it was not like the *hamin* of Shabbat that her mother makes.

She ran away from him and returned to her parents.

When she was asked: "Why did you come back? What did you lack?"

She said: "The *hamin*'s egg smells different, so I came back."

Discussion of
"THE TASTE OF THE SHABBAT'S *HAMIN*"

The storyteller, Simha Shamaka, was born in the 1930s in Libya. She immigrated to Israel in 1948. Twenty-five tales are registered in her name at IFA. She heard them in her childhood from her mother. This tale was filed in the archives in 1979.

This tale focuses on one of the *hamin* ingredients (*hamin*, or *cholent*, is a special dish in honor of Shabbat) representing the sacred time of Shabbat—the egg.[1] It is a hard-boiled egg cooked for a long time with the other components of *hamin*, becoming brown, very hard, and possessing a unique flavor (Ansky 2008, 30; Roden 1980, 101–2; Roden 1999a, 213; Marks 2010, 252–54). This method of cooking is already mentioned in the Rabbinical literature (Mishnah Shabbat 3:3; Jerusalem Talmud 3:3; Babylonian Talmud Shabbat 38b). The egg is used in the plot as a marker for maternal home and Jewish identity and is shown to have the power to bring back to Judaism a woman who converted to Islam. Quite a few tales deal with converted Jews who feel remorse when they smell, taste, or recall Jewish food, usually embodied by *cholent*.[2]

Indirectly, the tale also reflects the tension that existed in the Jewish society that lived as a minority group within Muslim society, such as the Jewish community in Libya, where the tale originated. The grave fear that Jewish society will be swallowed up in the alien one and will lose its

---

1 For more details about *hamin* (*cholent*), see the following tale and discussion.
2 For example: "What Brought Professor Vambery to Reflections of Repentance" (IFA 14762); "The Converts and the Taste of the *Cholent*" (IFA 23539); "Thanks to the Brown Eggs of the Shabbat" (IFA 23256).

identity is embodied here in the description of a Jewish girl who chooses to marry a Muslim man. In the tale, choosing a female figure to reflect society's weak points is understandable in light of the woman's place in Libyan Jewish society and the changes she underwent at the end of the nineteenth century and the beginning of the twentieth, when she had opportunities for education and integration into the workforce (Simon 1992).

This is also an etiological tale explaining a popular belief that *hamin* eggs save the soul and therefore it is not customary to give them to gentiles. Regarding the invitation of non-Jews to a Shabbat meal, there is already controversy in Rabbinical literature: "But he [R. Huna, who permits baking for heathens if a part thereof can be given to a child] disagrees with R. Joshua b. Levi; for R. Joshua b. Levi said: One may invite a heathen [to a meal] on a Shabbat, but one may not invite a heathen on a Festival as a preventive measure, lest he may [cook] more on his [the heathen's] account. R. Aha b. Jacob says: Not even on a Shabbat" (Babylonian Talmud Beitzah 21b).

The idea that the *hamin* egg is a unique dish reserved solely for Jews follows the entire plot. Later, the tale describes the longing of the Jewish woman who converted to Islam. This longing is awakened by the smell of the *hamin* that wafts on Shabbat from the Jewish households. The non-Jewish, caring husband worries about his wife's welfare, but does not fully understand the meaning of this food for his wife. In doing so, he actually does not understand her culture and her. This issue is present also among the Christian Armenians, who, as a people like the Jewish people, suffered persecution and extermination (Avakian and Haber 2005: 263).

The husband's solution to the problem is based on common sense. In his view, the way to overcome her longing is by preparing the same dish in his home. However, restoring the dish in the new "other" home does not solve anything. This failure stems not from the woman's inability to cook, but from her inability to bridge the representation and meaning of the *hamin* egg for her. The discrepancy between the dishes' fragrance does not derive from an objective physical fact but rather from an internal experience, the memories and emotional pool that compose her feelings of belonging and identity precisely during sacred time and through the foods that characterize it.[3] These are not accessible to her as long as she remains in the Muslim society, represented here by her husband's home. Therefore, the woman runs away from her husband and returns to her Jewish roots, explaining the reason for her actions in terms of the fragrance of the *hamin* egg, familiar to her from her maternal home. In this manner, the end of the tale connects to its opening: the *hamin* egg does indeed save a soul. The Jewish woman who almost lost her way returns home in the full sense of the word.

---

3 The connection of this tale to the midrash discussed in the introduction to this chapter, "The Taste of Shabbat," can be discerned. The common ground is the dish's special flavor due to its connection to sacred time.

THE ANGEL IN CHARGE OF THE SHOFAR BLASTS

IFA 11131

TOLD BY MR. LIVNI, RUSSIA
RECORDED BY ZEVULUN KORT

When God created the universe, he created with each and every thing an angel that would serve it and look after it. At that time, he created an angel in charge of the shofar blasts. Surely not every day of the year we blow the shofar, only on Rosh Hashanah. So throughout the year there is no role for the angel in charge of the blasts. Therefore, he was given a second role: to watch over the *hamin* on Shabbat.

And what if Rosh Hashanah falls on Shabbat? How would he watch the *hamin* and the blasts too? Therefore, he was given a dispensation. On Rosh Hashanah, the shofar is not blown so that he will be available and free to look after the *hamin*.

The angel is faithful in both his roles. When you want to make soup, you have to stand by the fire all the time and watch over it, if not the soup boils over, spills, and can extinguish the fire. As for the *hamin*, it is put in the oven for a whole day, and when taken out, it is nicely cooked.

Discussion of
"THE ANGEL IN CHARGE OF THE SHOFAR BLASTS"

There is no information about the storyteller, Mr. Livni, except that this tale is the only one registered in his name at IFA. It was filed in the archives in 1976.

This tale has etiological elements in it, one of which tries to explain why the shofar is not blown when Rosh Hashanah falls on Shabbat, both of which are sacred times. The basis for this ruling is the Mishnah and its interpretation in the Talmud (Mishnah Rosh Hashanah 4:1): "If the Festival of Rosh Hashanah occurred on Shabbat they used to blow the shofar in the Temple but not in the provinces. After the Temple was destroyed Rabban Yohanan ben Zakkai enacted that the shofar should be blown in any place that a Bet Din convened." (See also the Jerusalem Talmud, Rosh Hashanah 4:1.)

Versions of this tale are found in Hasidic literature from the nineteenth century.[1] At IFA, another version was also recorded forty years ago.[2] The tale is still told nowadays.[3] For example:

---

1 For example, in the book of R. Eliezer Zeev of Kretshnif (1880–1944), *Arbaa Arazim*, part 1, *Haezov, Parashat Vayishlah,*: "R. Itzhak of Rojin (1796–1850) said: The angel in charge of the shofar blasts, what does he do all year? And he explained that he is in charge of the 'Hamin' (Cholent), of every week of the year" (Kretshnif n.d.: 41).

2 Our tale was registered at IFA in 1976. Another version was recorded at IFA in 1980: "The Hamin Angel" (IFA 13064).

3 A version very close to the one here is on the website of the World Synagogue Association, "Shabbat," text 5, accessed December 29, 2020, https://hagabay .net/component/search/?searchword=%D7%AA%D7%A7%D7%99%D7

It is known that the *cholent* that the woman brings to the oven on Shabbat eve and brings it out on Shabbat is always good, and it is always tasty, not like other dishes that sometimes are tasty, and other times not. It is said that there is an angel who is in charged that the *cholent* pots will be tasty. And probably the same angel is in charge of the shofar blasts on Rosh Hashanah. The proof is—when Rosh Hashanah falls on Shabbat, the shofar is not blown because the same angel is busy at that time with the *cholent* pots of the Jews. (Nava Tehila Community, Givat Shmuel, Israel, newsletter no. 2, Dec. 23, 2011, p. 3)

The traditional explanation for the prohibition of blowing the shofar on Shabbat stems from the desire to refrain from moving the shofar from place to place (Babylonian Talmud, Rosh Hashanah 29b). Our tale offers a different, humorous explanation. The reason given is the inability of the appointed angel to perform two functions at the same time—one function is to keep the *cholent*, or *hamin*, from burning during the long hours of cooking, while the other is to watch over the person who is blowing the shofar, ensuring that he will succeed in this delicate duty. Blowing the shofar is not simple, and is accompanied by great tension both on the part of the performer and the audience. There are quite a few folktales dealing with the *baalei tkiyah*, the shofar blowers, who, on the holiday, in front of the entire community, fail to produce a proper sound.[4]

The idea of the inability of an angel to perform two roles at the same time is connected to the Rabbinical notion according to which an angel

---

%A2%D7%AA%20%D7%A9%D7%95%D7%A4%D7%A8&searchphrase =all&Itemid=244.

4 For example, the following tales, all of which deal with unsuccessful shofar blasts: "Ivan Will Blow the Shofar" (IFA 1643), where R. Levi Yitzchak of Berdichev is unable to get a sound from the shofar; "Tale for Rosh Hashanah" (IFA 5554), describing a rabbi who is unable to blow the shofar; "The Devil's Argument" (IFA 14714), in which the devil complains and accuses the person who is failing his mission to blow the shofar; "Advice to Unsuccessful Shofar Blower" (IFA 16187).

performs only one single mission (Bereshit Rabbah 50:2). Although this tale does not explicitly state that an angel does not perform two missions, this statement appears in the Hasidic version, as noted above. The belief that there are angels in charge of spiritual and physical aspects of our world was common in the Middle Ages in Europe. The roots of this notion are found in Rabbinical literature and even in the writings of the Second Temple period (Trachtenberg 1977, 68–69). The explicit tradition that there is an angel in charge of the shofar blasts originates also from the Middle Ages. The source is in the Hasidic circle of Ashkenaz from the twelfth century, but it is possible that they derived it from the first centuries CE Heichalot literature or were inspired by it (Liebes 1986, 19).

The tale is therefore based on three separate traditions, and binds them together: 1) an angel is in charge of shofar blasts, 2) an angel can perform only one mission, and 3) *hamin* is part of Shabbat delight.

The angel in the tale was given two tasks. The first is to ensure that the shofar blasts will succeed—blowing the shofar is carried out in the synagogue, which is the most sacred space for Jews, during one of the most sacred periods of the Jewish year—Rosh Hashanah. The purpose of the shofar blasts is to awaken God's mercy so that the gates of heaven will open. Therefore, the involvement of an angel in this act is of utmost importance. The second role is the supervision over the *hamin*. This idea is not based on a sacred tradition, but rather has a humorous aspect. Although *hamin* is associated with sacred time, it does not contain elements that are symbols of holiness.

Hamin is made in the kitchen, the intimate space of the woman, who has no role in Jewish public rituals. Her task on Shabbat is to bring to the table the very best dishes, dishes worthy of the day's sanctity. It falls to the angel to ensure that the *hamin* served to the diners on Shabbat will be optimally cooked even though people do not watch it. The proof that indeed an angel guards the *hamin* is presented in the tale by the comparison between *hamin* and soup: the latter should be constantly monitored so it will not boil over, while *hamin* is cooked unattended.

The great gap between the two roles of the angel, one in the realm of holiness, concerning the successful blowing of the shofar, and the other in the realm of the mundane, the supervision of the *hamin*, raises smiles among the audience. It is clear to all that *hamin* does not have any sanctified status. The humoristic interpretation given to a well-known halakhah is surprising and amuses the audience.

The End of a Blood Libel

IFA 10844

Told by Nehemia Varenbod, Russia
Recorded by Zalman Baharav

In the city of Boguslav, Ukraine, a *Shabbos goy* served in the homes of the Jews. He would remove the candles from the table on Shabbat, turn off the fire, turn on the samovar, and other such activities.

On Passover eve, the rabbi would sell him the *chametz*. For this work, Ivan the *Shabbos goy* would receive a few pennies, a glass of wine, a sweet Jewish challah, and sometimes even a stuffed fish, the craving of the Christian inhabitants of the town.

It was a hard winter at that time, and by the coming of spring the Jews were getting ready to celebrate Passover properly. But that year there was a shortage of horseradish, the bitter plant. How is it possible that this plant would not be present on the plate of the Seder table?

The rabbi and the heads of the community searched for the bitter herbs, the horseradish, and did not find any. The rabbi asked Ivan to travel to faraway villages to get horseradish no matter what, and promised to pay him whatever he would ask for. Ivan accepted this assignment, wandered around for a few days, and finally brought back several packages of this plant and received for each package ten kopecks, a decent amount back then. There was joy in Ivan's meager hut. Ivan's son, who went to visit his grandfather in a far village, took a bottle of vodka and a slice of Shabbat challah, but did not tell his father where he was going and when he would return.

A few days passed, Nikita the son disappeared, and his traces were not known. Ivan looked for his son who had gone missing, and told the police that Nikita, his oldest son, was gone, and the policeman told the priest. That is when the priest got an idea: since the Jewish Passover holiday is approaching, it means that the heads of the Jewish community have seized Ivan's son, drained his blood in order to put it in the matzot baked by the Jews. On Sunday, during the prayer service, he shared his assumption with the peasants and he sent Ivan to inform the villagers that the Jews had slaughtered his son, and to alert them to come to town and attack the Jews.

Ivan carried out his mission with faith, especially when he received some bottles of a bitter drink from the priest. Ivan returned to town from his mission and to the inn from the mission and, bitter about the loss of his son, went to the inn and got drunk and could not move away.

The night before, the son had dreamed that his father had died. He rushed to his father's place and did not find him. He realized that his father was in the tavern. The boy went out to the inn and found his father drunk as biblical Lot. He set his father on his feet, grabbed him with a firm arm as he walked through the market square, and supported his drunk father, so he would not fall in the middle of the square. At that moment, the priest appeared at the head of a gang equipped with axes and sacks to take the loot after robbing the Jewish shops. To their surprise, they saw Ivan and his son marching in the market square, and Ivan kissing his son, who had just returned from his grandfather's house in the village. The priest immediately scattered the crowd, who left the place in bitter disappointment, while the Jews rejoiced at the miracle that happened to them.

The priest called the Christian community's honorable leaders to the rabbi's house, who at the same time was sitting with his congregation, and begged him for forgiveness for the rude plot made by superstitious peasants (he said). The Christian leaders promised the rabbi they would maintain peace and good relations.

This is how the Jews of Boguslav were saved from destruction and slaughter.

Discussion of
"The End of a Blood Libel"

No information is provided about the storyteller, Nehemia Varen-bod, except that fifty-seven tales are registered in his name. This tale was filed in the archives in 1976.

Passover is a central sacred-time event in the Jewish calendar. Its main symbols are regeneration and rebirth, which reflect the changes that occur in nature during the spring season: new growth, sheep lambing, and barley ripening. Historically it marks the period of the Israelites' Exodus from Egypt, their transitioning from slavery to freedom, and their birth as the People of Israel. The Exodus from slavery to freedom involved much suffering and many dangers, as expressed in the verse, "Remember what Amalek did unto thee by the way, when ye were come forth out of Egypt" (Deuteronomy 25:17).

Over the generations, Passover became a time when the non-Jewish environment, especially the Christian one, found cause to clash with the Jews. The reason for this animosity can be attributed to the affinity the two religions have to the same sacred time. The Seder is mentioned in the New Testament as the Last Supper of Jesus with his disciples, during which the betrayal of Judas Iscariot that caused the death of Jesus was revealed (Luke 22:1–23; Matthew 26:14–29). The Eucharist, one of the sacraments of the Christian faith, in which the symbol of Christ's body is consumed and wine is drunk symbolizing the blood of Christ, symbolizes that feast as well (Corinthians 11:24–26; Luke 22:19–20). There is, therefore, a similarity and a family connection between the two separate rituals (Feeley-Harnick 1994). On Pesach, the Jews eat matzah and drink wine, and in the Christian Eucharist they eat the host (a wafer similar to matzah) and drink wine. This similarity was a source of conflict, perhaps out of a desire to be different.[1]

Therefore, new Jewish symbolic significance was added to Passover—of the calamities and persecutions that were a plight of the Jewish Diaspora throughout their exile. The memory of riots and persecutions was assimilated into folktales. For example, the oicotype on blood libel:[2]

AT *730 F (IFA) Blood Libel: A Missing Child Is Found Alive

I. Jew baiters hide a non-Jewish child, on the eve of Passover, or it gets lost. The Jews are accused of murdering the child for ritual use of its blood.

II. The child is found alive by coincidence. The Jewish community is saved, the slanderers condemned.

Often in folktales, Jews were accused of murdering Christian children and using their blood to bake matzot before Passover.[3] The researcher Alan Dandes ascribed the many blood libels in which the Jews were accused specifically on Passover to what he calls "projective inversion." In his view, the Eucharist ritual is a sort of symbolic cannibalism. The guilt it inspires is cast collectively on the Jews, being the "other" group, and ideal as a scapegoat. The Jews are now the ones charged with murder for ceremonial use of blood (Dundes 1991, 354).

The setting of this tale is realistic: the city of Boguslav, the Yiddish name for the city of Bohuslav in the Kiev region, is in the center of Ukraine,

1 For further discussion on this issue, see Yuval 2008.
2 For discussion of this oicotype, see Bar-Itzhak 2008, 228.
3 For an extensive survey of the blood libels associated with the baking of matzot on Passover in folktales, especially in the nineteenth and twentieth centuries, see Dundes 1991; Bar-Itzhak 2008. On its ancient sources and research on the subject, see Ben-Amos 2006–11, 3:31–33. For a discussion of a folktale about blood libel from the IFA collection, see Rudin 2008. On drinking blood as a form of strange eating, see Shahani 2018.

49°32′48″N, 30°52′22″E. At the beginning of the twentieth century, Jews accounted for more than half of the city's population.[4] There Jews suffered severe recurrent persecutions beginning in the seventeenth century, especially the Khmelnitsky pogroms. In the course of the eighteenth century they experienced the Cossacks riots and the Haidamak pogroms (Clier 2011). In 1918–20 there were riots in the city.[5]

Central to the tale are fear of harm befalling the community and threats to Jewish life. These are channeled into a ritual symbol, the bitter herb, which on Passover is a reminder of the suffering and bitter life of the Israelites who were slaves in Egypt before their establishment as a people. The bitter herb mentioned in the tale, symbolizing historical suffering, is also the cause in the present of embittering many Jewish and non-Jewish lives alike. In the plot, expressions related to the word *bitter* occur five times: *bitter herb* is mentioned twice, the *bitter drink* drunk by gentiles, the *bitter soul* of the gentile father who is persuaded his son was murdered by the same Jews he served faithfully, and in the name of the inn where the son finds his drunk father. The Hebrew word the narrator chose for "inn" is *Bet Marzeah*, in which appears the syllable *mar*, which means bitter. Although this term is not related to the meaning of the expression "bitter," it is possible that the narrator chose it unconsciously because of the sound—the syllable *mar* at the beginning of the word—when in two other occurrences he used the Hebrew term *pundak* to refer to the inn.

The plot revolves around the complex relations between the Jews and their non-Jewish neighbors. At first, their interactions are described as stable and safe for the Jews. The gentile identified later in the plot by his first name, Ivan, serves the Jews mainly during their sacred time: on

---

4 "Boguslav, Ukraine," Jewish Virtual Library, accessed December 29, 2020, http://www.jewishvirtuallibrary.org/jsource/judaica/ejud_0002_0004_0_03251.html.

5 See personal testimony (Korut 1923, 140–41).

Shabbat and Passover. The Jews, for their part, reward him with a drink, money, and Jewish culinary delicacies: sweet fish and sweet challah. The sweet taste reflects the good relations between the two religions. This taste is diametrically opposed to the bitter taste that lies at the center of the plot and symbolizes the impaired relations between them. This balance is breached after the Jews send the gentile to get the bitter herb.[6] For the first time, they send him on a mission they are able to perform on their own. Until then, they asked him to exclusively perform tasks that they themselves could not do without desecrating sacred time: Shabbat and Passover. The tale does not provide a convincing reason why the Jews did not seek the bitter herbs themselves. The difficulty of the task is not a convincing enough reason. The gentile, on the other hand, does not avoid the great effort involved in searching for the bitter herbs, and he succeeds. It seems that the Jews' nonaction is a flaw, since it brings calamity both to the Jews and to the gentiles.

The bitter herbs the Jews sought for the holiday are loaded with symbolic implications. The gentile who went to get the bitter herbs for the Jews eventually caused the "embittering" of their lives. The bitter herbs also hurt the gentile himself, who believed the priest who accused the Jews of murdering his son. The delicate relations between the Jewish community and their non-Jewish neighbors were damaged, spreading distrust. Jews feared for their lives, but the gentiles, too, feared being harmed by them: according to their own legends, Jews might abduct a gentile child and use his blood to

---

6 A mission in search of a particular type of food is a well-known motif in folk-tales (H 1305, Quest for the Best of Bread; H 1305.1, Quest for the Best of Meat; H1305.2, Quest for Best-Cooked Dish), as well as in the tale type ATU 402, where the acquisition of food often leads to a positive development in the plot, while in our tale gaining it produces a calamity. See, for example, a search for tiny bread, in the tale "The King's Son and the Girl from the Pumpkin" (IFA 4697).

bake matzah for Passover.[7] Eventually, in the tale, the mutual fears dissipate. It is proven that the Jews did not kidnap the gentile child, who was found safe and sound, and the threat of riots, as an act of revenge, is removed. Jews are assured of the restoration of normal neighborly relations, and they can safely celebrate Passover.

7　The belief that matzah is made with blood is rooted and present even in the modern age. For example, in the tale "Matzah for the Gentiles" (IFA 23685), the narrator describes how, as a very young girl in school, while eating matzah on Passover, another pupil claimed it was baked with Christian blood.

Wherefore the Custom of Eating Dairy Products on Shavuot

IFA 388

Told and recorded by
Haim Dov Armon, Poland

In Vilna, the "Jerusalem of Lithuania," there were women scholars too, women who were well versed in the "small print" of our literature.

Once Fruma, the well-known righteous and learned spouse of Reb Leib, raised her voice to say: "How long? Can it be written in the Torah 'And he will rule over you', and we will stand by and be silent? This situation should end! It must be changed at last and the text should be amended to 'She will rule over him!'"

In the large women's section at the synagogue, a gathering of women took place. They wiped a tear from their eyes and unanimously announced: "Fruma the righteous is right!"

The truth is that most of the women did not even understand what was in question, but it was already a habit for them, if righteous Fruma pleads, it is surely assumed that her words are true and correct. In short, the modest women of Vilna suddenly became fighters for women's equal rights.

Fruma suggested going on strike. This was exactly during the week of Shavuot, when the Torah was given. These arrogant men should feel the "taste" of the holiday when there is no work on our part. We women, on whose shoulders the most severe and harsh commandments were imposed will all strike. On Shavuot, any woman should dare cook and bake, not a dish or a pastry!

They said and so did. They came home, wore holiday clothes, did not bother in the kitchen, did not prepare fish or meat, did not bake challah. In short, this was a severe protest strike with the slogan: "And she will rule over him."

Reb Leib returned home after the long prayer, and what does he see before him? The table is not set and his righteous wife Fruma is holding a strike, precisely on the holiday. Reb Leib thought: Could it be, Heaven forbid, she's lost her mind? Maybe silliness came upon her. It must be because I have sinned in something and punishment from Heaven comes upon me. . . .

To relax a little, he smoked his pipe (it's okay to smoke on this holiday!) and went out to get some fresh air instead of food. Walking like this in front of his house, Reb Leib noticed that other men were also walking, just like him. However, no one said a word to the other. It had to be that they decided to accept the suffering with love so as not to violate the sanctity of the holiday.

Yankel the wagon driver also came out, as did Yoshe the porter, "Happy holiday!"

"Oh, for God's sake," answered Yoshe, "What happy holiday for you?" My old lady went crazy and did not prepare the holiday.

"Ah, my old lady went crazy too," Yankel answered loudly.

The other men, hearing the dialogue between Yankel and Yoshe, realized that it was not simple. This was an unusual event, some kind of a well-organized rebellion.

What is the opinion of the rabbi on this matter? Most of them turned to Reb Leib. Because if there is rebellion and revolution of women here, it is clear that the driving force behind it is Fruma, the wife of Reb Leib!

The rabbi ordered someone to summon Fruma. Adorned and accompanied by two other women, Fruma stood before her husband.

"What is this?" asks the old rabbi, turning to Fruma.

"We women demand that the harsh and severe commandments that have burdened our weak shoulders for generations should be removed. We mean specifically the rule 'And he will rule over you.' It must be corrected to 'And she will rule over him,' and if not, with all due respect, you men go and become homemakers for yourselves!"

The old rabbi heard his wife's complaints, his eyes closed. "Right, right, but we too, men, have demands. If the strike does not stop immediately, we will cancel the ban ordered by Rabbi Gershom *Me'or Hagolah* (Light of the Diaspora). From now on it will be permissible for any man to marry another wife or more."

Hearing that, Reb Leib's wife turned pale and ran along with the other women to prepare the holiday meal. Since there was not a piece of meat or fish, they soon caught a piece of dough from here and a piece of cheese from there and made dairy pancakes. Since then, the custom has been to prepare dairy dishes for Shavuot. And the world continues to follow the directive: "And he will rule over her!"

"Wherefore the Custom of Eating Dairy Products on Shavuot"

No information is provided for the storyteller, Haim Dov Armon, except that twelve tales are registered in his name at IFA. This tale was filed in 1958.

This tale is an etiological novella that seeks to explain why dairy foods are served on Shavuot.[1] In the halakhah (the traditional body of Jewish laws) there is a controversy regarding the eating of dairy products on Shavuot. According to one commentary, the joy of the holiday is expressed in eating meat and drinking wine (Maimonides, *Mishneh Torah*, Laws of Yom Tov, 6:17–18). According to Maimonides' assertion, some claimed that on Shavuot one should first eat dairy foods and then eat meat.[2]

The conclusion of our tale presents the dairy menu of the holiday as a flaw, a privation due to the undermining of the existing order between the sexes. This order is said to be anchored in the determination "and he shall rule over thee" (Genesis 3:16). The biblical verse regulates the relationship between Adam and Eve after they were expelled from the Garden of Eden and serves as a model for all humanity. It is the world order determined by God the Creator and in the eyes of his believers is the optimal one. Defying it damaged the foundations of society and the world.

---

1 For details on the dispute and the various opinions, see Farkash 1996.
2 On the issue of separating milk from meat according to rules of kashrut, see the introduction to chapter 4.

Shavuot is one of the three major festivals mentioned in the Torah (Exodus 23:14–19) along with Pesach and Sukkot. As mentioned in the introduction to this chapter, these three festivals are also markers of major events in the yearly agricultural cycle: barley harvesting in the spring coinciding with Pesach, appearance of the first fruits in early summer with Shavuot, and harvest of the fall crops with Sukkot. They also celebrate major chapters in the early history of the nation: the Exodus from Egypt celebrated on Pesach, receiving the Torah on Shavuot, and forty years of wandering in the desert on Sukkot. In our tale, the narrator seems to expect that there ought to be a festive menu to express the importance of Shavuot.

Food served during a holiday is supposed to express its importance and holiness and is usually characterized by the following attributes. First, the food served is expensive and is not a part of the usual daily menu. Second, great time and effort are invested in preparing the food. Third, cooking time is prolonged. The longer it cooks, the more it is considered to have been removed from its original, "wild" state, becoming closer to culture and more fit for human consumption.[3]

In this tale, the milk pancakes prepared on Shavuot are not characterized by the qualities presented above: they were prepared from dough and milk, which are common and cheap products used daily, as opposed to meat and fish that according to the tale were not available. The pancakes were not meticulously prepared; on the contrary, they were prepared hastily and carelessly; as the narrator says, "they soon caught a piece of dough from here and a piece of cheese from there." Finally, cooking the pancakes did not take long. After all, it is said that there was no time left to prepare meat and fish before the holiday started.

Food preparation and the serving of it in Jewish society are tasks imposed on women. The dairy menu served by the women reflects the disruption of the desired gender order. For if the women were to perform their duties

---

3 According to the anthropologist Claude Lévi-Strauss's models; see introduction to this chapter.

properly, they would have prepared a meal that included meat. The disruption stems from the strike, and even "rebellion," that the women conducted in order to protest their "natural" place in society. The women protested over being ruled by men and sought to alter this situation by not preparing the holiday dishes. The women's revolt is reminiscent of the Lilith myth, the first woman to demand equality, rebelling and becoming the enemy of wives and proper mothers (Pintel-Ginsberg 2013, 333–34). It is also a kind of refinement of the famous women's strike of nonmarital relations which is at the center of the play *Lysistrata*, (first performed in 411 BCE), the comedy by the classical Greek playwright Aristophanes.[4]

Through our tale, the narrator expresses his worldview regarding the proper place of women in society. According to him, the undermining of this order stems from women's book learning, common in Vilna (the "Jerusalem of Lithuania").[5] The name of the city is not necessarily a realistic detail, although there are some testimonies that can reinforce the claim that there were erudite women in Vilna. Advanced education among women in Jewish society was not uncommon in Poland, Russia, and Belarus. Actually, Lithuania was more conservative in this regard, but there were well-known cases of well-educated women in Vilna, such as Esther Rubinstein (1883–1924), who was famous for her knowledge of Talmud and modern Hebrew literature (Greenbaum, 5).

The city's name may be mentioned in order to point out the danger inherent in the precedent. If the women's rebellion broke out in Vilna, a major city of Jewish Eastern Europe, it might possibly inspire emulation and dissemination throughout the Jewish world. As the narrator sees it, women's erudition is dangerous. Their knowledge of traditional texts, or in his words "the small print of our literature," is liable to harm the

---

4 On the close connection between food and marital relations, see chapter 2. The comedy *Lysistrata* has been adapted for many years for stage and screen. A recent version is the 2011 French film *La source des femmes*, directed by Radu Mihaileanu.

5 On the centrality of Vilna in Eastern European Jewish world, see Ran 1987.

society's proper order and family integrity. The narrator does not explain what he means by "small print." The term exists in Hebrew: *otiot zeira*, letters written in the Torah smaller than the rest. But it seems that this is not his intention. It is possible that his words are directed to the less central interpretations that appear in printed Talmud in small letters. If this is the intention, it means that the women were also familiar with these interpretations or, pejoratively, they did not differentiate between these and the major traditional commentaries.

Women's focus on the small letters is the source of the error. They seek to change the content of the Torah verses, but they lack the basic insight—it is impossible to alter the Torah, not even for the slightest change. Their demand to change the verse "and he will rule over you" to "she will rule" stems from the woman's inability to understand in depth the foundations of the Torah.

At first, the conflict between the sexes seems to have been won in favor of the women. The men emerge from inside their homes, the private space in which the festival is supposed to be celebrated, into the open space. This space differs not only from the domestic and private one, but also from the sacred public space, which is the synagogue, from which the men returned from the holiday and where (in the women's section) the women's organization began under the leadership of Rabbi Leib's wife. It is difficult to determine if Rabbi Leib is a real historical figure because there were two rabbis in Vilna named Rabbi Aryeh Leib Shapira: the grandfather (1701–61), and his grandson (1787–1853). It is not known what their wives' names were.

The street where the men walk helplessly and smoke is a no-man's-land. The men were "thrown" from their homes by the women's strike. Thus the conflict in the plot is resolved in two stages: In the first one, there is an open confrontation between Rabbi Leib and his wife Fruma (the two represent the different genders) in the no-man's-land—in the street for all to see. Fruma presents in public the women's demand to change the world order, and requests on behalf of all women that the burden of the difficult commandments be removed and that the law "And he will rule over you" be amended. The tale does not mention what harsh commandments are imposed on women, but the answer can be found in the verse itself—"Unto the woman he said, I will greatly multiply thy sorrow and thy conception; in sorrow thou shalt bring forth children; and thy desire shall be to thy husband, and he shall rule over thee" (Genesis 3:16)—and in the solution devised by the rabbi.

According to the verse, the yoke of women's mitzvot is the difficulties of giving birth and women's need for men. The rabbi's reply to the women relates directly to this verse by annulling the rabbinical prohibition of polygamy by Gershom Me'or Hagolah, the head of the Jewish community in the eleventh century in Mainz, Germany (*Aruch Hashulchan* Even Ezer, divorce ruling 145). This annulment means granting permission to marry multiple women. The new wives will be able to give birth instead of the current ones and will even cook for the men. The rabbi's proposal turns the tables by suggesting that the men will no longer have marital relations with their wives and that food will be provided to them by other women. The threat is reminiscent of an ancient source describing Eve conversing with Adam: "R. Simlai said: She came upon him with her answers all ready, saying to him, 'What think you: that I will die and another Eve will be created for you?'" (Genesis Rabbah 19:5).

The proposal terrifies the women, evokes their jealousy, and puts an end to the strike. The women return to their "natural" place, according to the narrator, going back to their kitchens and preparing the food. This food, put together hastily and with everyday ingredients, set the tradition of eating dairy foods on Shavuot. Had the proper and intended social order been preserved, the holiday would have been celebrated with meat and fish dishes, as befits a central festival.

EPILOGUE

E ach of the thirty tales compiled in this book represents a whole wide world. Every one of them hoards memories of former generations as well as enlightened and profound insights about life, human nature, and humans' complex relationships with their surroundings. Although these tales have been told in different languages by distinct ethnic groups and belong to different literary genres, they have one common element: the food representations woven into their plots.

Food is foundational to human experience, one of the most familiar ingredients of a person's life since birth and, as some believe, even from the moment of our creation. Its physical aspects are well known to us, acting on all of our senses, and have a profound impact on our emotional world. Since food is deeply embedded in personal and group memory, it is easy to use it as an image and a universal, unmediated language of signs and symbols. This language, which is so deeply ingrained in us, intensifies the issues that are intertwined in the tales. Sometimes it provides the most dramatic representations and images, such as the description of a desperate, hungry, meager person who smells dishes he cannot afford himself, or of bountiful delicacies women heap on their loved ones. This language of signs, sometimes resonating with dramatic intensity, allows narrators to approach sensitive and charged subjects that occupy their audience, and through food to discuss different and deeper issues.

The tales included in this book venture into a variety of areas: some deal with the sensory aspect of food, its pleasures and appropriate limits. Some examine the complexity of gender relations, others allow a critical examination of social relations and the manner in which moral values are implemented. Some tales treat sensitive issues of the Jewish faith, like food dividing Jews from surrounding non-Jewish communities. Other tales reflect on Jewish sacred time and society's attitude toward it. In many there is criticism, at times uncompromising and self-mocking, of the reality created by people's weaknesses and strengths.

A comprehensive and unifying examination of the tales assembled in this book enables one to discern the common themes that have preoccupied Jewish culture for centuries. Prominent is the existential need to maintain identity, whether it be personal or gender, as well as collective identity as a minority group struggling to survive. Also notable is the group's deep fear of annihilation, both cultural (due to assimilation or the inability to maintain its customs and beliefs) and physical (caused by a life-threatening environment), a fear grounded in history and diaspora experience as the Jewish people suffered from forced religious conversion, expulsion, and persecution, horrifically culminating in the Holocaust.

Another prominent issue in examining the complete collection is the tales' centrality as bearers of memory. They commemorate a world that no longer exists, whether because of the obliteration of entire Jewish communities in the Holocaust or the disappearance of the Jewish communities in the Arab world after the establishment of the State of Israel. The tales presented here seek to commemorate the special taste of unique foods, the social relations within the community that shares meals, and the special dishes that have accompanied different periods of the Jewish life cycle and its holidays. Above all, they commemorate the memory of the foods tastes and the pleasures they invoke.

This book offers scholarly commentaries and annotations, but the tales can stand alone. They offer a window into the lives of the people who told them. By exploring their meanings, one can better understand the worlds in which those storytellers lived, giving us insight into how and why food was central, not only to the tales, but also to cultural existence.

Ultimately the tales of this book are its core, with their eternal taste and aroma.

Appendix.
List of the Tales

IFA Tale	Narrator	Country	Recorder	Tale Type
IFA 178—The Price of Smelling	Sa'id Kafia	Yemen	Yihia Yihia	ATU 1804B, AT 1804B Payment with the Clink of Money
IFA 388—Wherefore the Custom of Eating Dairy Products on Shavuot	Haim Dov Armon	Poland	Haim Dov Armon	
IFA 2400—Hosts Who do Not Feed Their Guest	Shemuel Rekanati	Sephardic, Israel	Rachel Seri	ATU 1568* The Master and the Farmhand at the Table
IFA 3060—There Is No Trust in a Gentile Even after Forty Years	Flora Cohen	Egypt	Ilana Zohar	AT 910*M, Do Not Believe a Gentile, Even Forty Years after His Death
IFA 3346—Christian Hell and Jewish Hell	Berl Rabinovitch	Belarus	Zalman Baharav	ATU 821 B* The Long Spoons, AT 821 B* Devil as Host at Dinner
IFA 4515—Diet	Hugo Haim Mustaki	Italy	Menahem ben Arieh	

IFA Tale	Narrator	Country	Recorder	Tale Type
IFA 5066—Woman Raises, Woman Lowers, a Man's Honor Is in a Woman's Hands	Shlomo Hazan	Morocco	Yitshak Wechsler	ATU 923B, AT 923B The Princess Who Was Responsible for Her Own Fortune
IFA 5691—Love Like Salt	Serl Haimovits	Poland	Zvi Moshe Haimovits	ATU 923 Love Like Salt
IFA 5872—The Bride Who Knew It All	Moshe Nehmad	Persia	Moshe Nehmad	AT 1328*-* (IFA) A Woman Does Not Know Her Housework
IFA 6110—The Jewish Rabbi and the King	David Perez	Morocco	Yihia Perez	
IFA 6437— R. Eliyahu Buhbut and the Fish on Shabbat Eve	Yosef Mashash	Morocco	Moshe Rabi	
IFA 9127—Who Will Be the Baal Shem Tov's Neighbor in the World to Come?	Malka Herts	Ukraine	Yifrah Haviv	AT 809*-*A (IFA) The Companion in Paradise
IFA 9782—*Batel Bashishim*— One-Sixtieth Is Negligible	Raphael Cohen	Lithuania	Malka Cohen	
IFA 10660—The Butter Cake of Pasha-Leah	Hannah Shneid	Poland	Avraham Keren	
IFA 10844—The End of a Blood Libel	Nehemia Varenbod	Russia	Zalman Baharav	AT *730 F (IFA) Blood Libel: A missing child is found alive

IFA Tale	Narrator	Country	Recorder	Tale Type
IFA 11131—The Angel in Charge of the Shofar Blasts	Mr. Livni	Russia	Zevulun Kort	
IFA 11180—Three Great Mitzvot	Avraham Keren	Poland	Avraham Keren	
IFA 12396—The Taste of the Shabbat's Hamin	Simha Shamaka	Libya	Rivka Peer and Penina Resnik	
IFA 12582—Poor Man's Beans	Camelia Shahar-Russo	Turkey	Tamar Alexander	
IFA 13362— R. Israel Avidani in the Ishmaelite Town	Aluan Avidani	Kurdistan Iraq	Aluan Avidani	
IFA 13385— A Guest for Shabbat	Mordechai Hillel Kroshnitz	Poland	Ayelet Etinger	
IFA 14221— Home-Cooked Food	Mordechai Hillel Kroshnitz	Poland	Ayelet Etinger	
IFA 14701—Stone Soup	Hemda Shaham	Bulgaria	Yifrah Haviv	ATU 1548 The Soup-Stone AT 1548 The Soup-Stone Needs Only the Addition of a Few Vegetables and a Bit of Meat
IFA 15354—The Second-Rate Challah	Leah Blusher	Lithuania	Carmela Blusher	
IFA 16176—The Rebbe and Worldly Pleasures	Alexander Andzel	Poland	Avraham Keren	AT 1533 The Wise Carving of the Fowl

IFA Tale	Narrator	Country	Recorder	Tale Type
IFA 16648—The Way to Become Rich	Shimon Kbarnit Likbornik	Russia	Shimon Kbarnit Likbornik	
IFA 17230— Big Eyes	Peninah Feldman	Argentina	Yifrah Haviv	
IFA 20195—If Only You Knew the Taste	Shela Aranya	Turkey	Matilda Coen-Sarano	ATU 1855D You Do Not Know What You Are Missing
IFA 22813—The Boundaries of Craving	Miriam Aharon Azriel	Yemen	Miriam Aharon Azriel	AT 1533 The Wise Carving of the Fowl
IFA 22918—No Answers Are Given But by Women	Haji Firji Naji Abu Raya	Muslim, Israel	Joram Meron	

BIBLIOGRAPHY

Aarne, Antti. 1964. *The Types of the Folktale.* Edited by Stith Thompson. Helsinki: Suomalainen Tiedeakatemia.

Albala, Ken. 2007. *Beans: A History.* Oxford: Berg.

Alexander, Tamar. 1981. "A Neighbour in Paradise in the Book of the Pious—A Traditional Folktale in an Ideological Context." [In Hebrew.] *Jerusalem Studies in Jewish Folklore* 1 (1981): 61–82.

———. 1999. *The Beloved Friend-and-a-Half: Studies in Sephardic Folk Literature.* [In Hebrew.] Jerusalem: Magnes Press, Hebrew University, and Ben-Gurion University Press.

———. 2008. *The Heart Is a Mirror: The Sephardic Folktale.* Detroit, MI: Wayne State University Press.

Alexander, Tamar, and Dov Noy. 1989. *The Treasure of Our Fathers, 100 Judeo-Spanish Tales.* [In Hebrew.] Jerusalem: Misgav Yerushalayim, Hebrew University.

Ansky, Sherry. 2008. *Tscholent.* [In Hebrew.] Jerusalem: Keter.

Archer, Jane E., Richard Marggraf Turley, and Howard Thomas. 2014. *Food and the Literary Imagination.* Hampshire, UK: Palgrave Macmillan.

Avakian, Arlene Voski, ed. 1997. *Through the Kitchen Window: Women Explore the Intimate Meanings of Food and Cooking.* Boston: Beacon Press.

Avakian, Arlene Voski, and Barbara Haber, eds. 2005. *From Betty Crocker to Feminist Food Studies: Critical Perspectives on Women and Food.* Amherst: University of Massachusetts Press.

Bahloul, Joëlle. 1983. *Le Culte de la table dressée: Rites et traditions de la table juive algérienne.* Paris: Editions A. M. Métailié.

Baik, Byung-Kee, and Steven E. Ullrich. 2008. "Barley for Food: Characteristics, Improvement, and Renewed Interest." *Journal of Cereal Science* 48, no. 2: 233–42.

Bar-Itzhak, Haya. 1987. "'Saint's Legend' as a Genre in Jewish Folk Literature (Sample of Oral Stories about Rabbi Israel Baal-Shem Tov, Rabbi Chaim Pinto and Rabbi Shalom Shabazi)." [In Hebrew.] PhD diss., Hebrew University.

———. 1993. "'Smeda Rmeda Who Destroys Her Luck with Her Own Hands': A Jewish Moroccan Cinderella Tale in an Israeli Context." *Journal of Folklore Research* 30, nos. 2/3 (1993): 93–125.

———. 2001. *Jewish Poland—Legends of Origin*. Detroit, MI: Wayne State University Press.

———. 2008. "Women in Blood Libel Legends of Polish Jews—The Legend about Adil Kikinish from Drohobych." [In Hebrew.] *Chuliyot* 11: 227–35.

———. 2013. "Folk Narratives in Israel." In *Encyclopedia of Jewish Folklore and Traditions*, edited by Haya Bar-Itzhak, 1:176–78. New York: M. E. Sharpe.

———. 2019. "The Israel Folktale Archives and the Preservation of the Cultural Heritage in Israel." Introduction to *The Power of a Tale*, edited by Haya Bar-Itzhak and Idit Pintel-Ginsberg, xxiii–xxxii. Detroit: Wayne State University Press.

Bar-Itzhak, Haya, and Idit Pintel-Ginsberg. 2019. *The Power of a Tale*. Detroit, MI: Wayne State University Press.

Bar-Itzhak, Haya, and Aliza Shenhar. 1993a. *Jewish Moroccan Folk Narratives from Israel*. Detroit, MI: Wayne State University Press.

———. 1993b. "Processes of Change in Israeli Society as Reflected in Folklore Research: The Beit-She'an Model." *Jewish Folklore and Ethnology Review* 15: 128–33.

Barthes, Roland. 1957. *Mythologies*. Paris: Editions du Seuil.

———. 1961. "Pour une psycho-sociologie de l'alimentation contemporaine." *Annales: Économies, Sociétés, Civilisations* 16: 977–86.

Ben-Amos, Dan. 1992. "Folktale." In *Folklore, Cultural Performances, and Popular Entertainments*, edited by Richard Bauman, 101–18. New York: Oxford University Press.

———. 2006–11. *Folktales of the Jews.* 3 vols. Philadelphia: The Jewish Publication Society.

Ben Simhon, Raphael. 1998. *North African Judaism, Customs, and Practices around the Year.* [In Hebrew.] Jerusalem: Bnei Issachar Institute.

Ben-Yossef, No'am, ed. 2006. *Bread: Daily and Divine.* Jerusalem: Israel Museum.

Bergson, Henri. 1983. *Le Rire.* Paris: Quadrige/Puf.

———. 1999. *Laughter: An Essay on the Meaning of the Comic.* Translated by Cloudesley Brereton and Fred Rothwell. First published Macmillan, 1911. Project Gutenberg. https://www.gutenberg.org/files/4352/4352-h/4352-h.htm.

Bourdieu, Pierre. 1984. *Distinction: A Social Critique of the Judgement of Taste.* Cambridge, MA: Harvard University Press.

Brulotte, Ronda, and Michael A. Di Giovine, eds. 2014. *Edible Identities: Food as Cultural Heritage.* Burlington, VT: Ashgate.

Buber, Martin. 1965. *Or Haganuz.* [In Hebrew.] Jerusalem: Schocken.

Butler, Judith. 1990. *Gender Trouble.* New York: Routledge.

Bynum, Caroline Walker. 1987. *Holy Feast and Holy Fast: The Religious Significance of Food to Medieval Women.* Berkeley: University of California Press.

Chang, Isabelle C. 1969. *Tales from Old China.* New York: Random House.

Charles, Nickie, and Marion Kerr. 1988. *Women, Food and Families.* Manchester, UK: Manchester University Press.

Classen, Constance, David Howes, and Anthony Synnot. 1994. *Aroma: The Cultural History of Smell.* London: Routledge.

Cohen Ferris, Marcie. 2015. "Feeding the Jewish Soul in the Delta Diaspora." In *The Food and Folklore Reader,* edited by Lucy Long, 135–45. London: Bloomsbury Academic.

Cooper, John. 1993. *Eat and Be Satisfied: A Social History of Jewish Food.* Northwale, NJ: Jason Aronson.

Counihan, Carole M. 1999. *The Anthropology of Food and Body: Gender, Meaning, and Power.* New York: Routledge.

Counihan, Carole M., and Steven L. Kaplan. 1998. *Food and Gender.* Ajanta, India: Harwood Academic Publishers.

Crane, Ethel Eva. 1999. *The World History of Beekeeping and Honey Hunting*. New York: Routledge.

Dahamshe, Amer. 2017. *A Local Habitation and a Name*. [In Hebrew.] Beer Sheva, Israel: Ben Gurion University and Modi'in, Israel: Kinneret Zmora-Bitan, Dvir.

Dan, Joseph. 1974. *The Hebrew Story in the Middle Ages*. [In Hebrew.] Jerusalem: Keter.

———. 1975. *Ethical and Homiletical Literature*. [In Hebrew.] Jerusalem: Keter.

Delany, Joseph. 1909. "Gluttony." In *The Catholic Encyclopedia*, vol. 6. New York: Robert Appleton.

De Silva, Cara, ed. 2006. *In Memory's Kitchen*. Lanham, MD: Rowman and Littlefield.

Desmet, Pieter M. A., and Hendrik N. J. Schifferstein. 2008. "Sources of Positive and Negative Emotions in Food Experience." *Appetite* 50: 290–301.

DeVault, Marjorie. 1991. *Feeding the Family: The Social Organization of Caring as Gendered Work*. Chicago: University of Chicago Press.

Diner, Hasia R. 2002. *Hungering for America: Italian, Irish, and Jewish Foodways in the Age of Migration*. Cambridge, MA: Harvard University Press.

Douglas, Mary. 1966. *Purity and Danger*. London: Routledge.

———. 1984. *Food in the Social Order: Studies of Food and Festivities in Three American Communities*. London: Routledge.

———. 1997. "Deciphering a Meal." In *Food and Culture*, edited by Carole Counihan and Penny Van Esterik. New York: Routledge.

Druyanov, Alter. 1963. *The Book of Jokes and Witticisms*. [In Hebrew.] Tel Aviv: Dvir.

Dundes, Alan. 1983. "'To Love My Father All': A Psychoanalytic Study of the Folktale Source of King Lear." In *Cinderella: A Casebook*, edited by Alan Dundes, 229–44. New York: Wildman Press.

———. 1991. "The Ritual Murder of Blood Libel Legend: A Study of Anti-Semitic Victimization through Projective Inversion." In *The Blood Libel Legend: A Casebook in Anti-Semitic Folklore*, edited by Alan Dundes, 336–76. Madison: University of Wisconsin Press.

Durkheim, Emile. 1971. *The Elementary Forms of the Religious Life*. London: George Allen and Unwin.

Dvir-Goldberg, Rivka. 2003. *The Zaddik and the Palace of Leviathan: A Study of Hasidic Tales Told by Zaddikim*. [In Hebrew.] Tel Aviv: Hakibbutz Hameuchad.

Eisenstein, Judah David. 1969. *Otzar Midrashim* [Anthology of midrashim]. 2 vols. Bibliotheca Midraschica.

Eliade, Mircea. 1965. *Le sacré et le profane*. Paris: Gallimard.

Farkash, Yossi. 1996. "The Custom of Eating Dairy Products on Shavuot." [In Hebrew.] *Be Sdeh Hemed* 5–6.

Feeley-Harnik, Gillian. 1981. *The Lord's Table: Eucharist and Passover in Early Christianity*. Philadelphia: University of Pennsylvania Press.

———. 1994. *The Lord's Table: The Meaning of Food in Early Judaism and Christianity*. Washington, DC: Smithsonian Institution Press.

Fialkova, Larisa, and Elenevskaya, Maria. 2007. *Ex-Soviets in Israel: From Personal Narratives to a Group Portrait*. Detroit, MI: Wayne State University Press.

Fischler, Claude. 1988. "Food, Self and Identity." *Social Science Information* 27, no. 2: 275–92.

Friedlander, Judith. 1986. "Jewish Cooking in the American Melting-Pot." *Revue française d'études américaines* 27/28 (February 1986): 87–98.

Friedlander, Michael, trans. 1904. *The Guide for the Perplexed*, by Moses Maimonides. New York: E. P. Dutton.

Gaon, Moshe David. 1928. *Oriental Jews in Eretz Yisrael*. Vol. 1. [In Hebrew.] Jerusalem: Azriel.

Gardner, Gregg. 2015. *The Origins of Organized Charity in Rabbinic Judaism*. Cambridge: Cambridge University Press.

Gaster, Theodor. 1961. *Thespis: Ritual, Myth and Drama in the Ancient Near East*. Garden City, NY: Doubleday.

German, Kathleen M. 2011. "Memory, Identity, and Resistance: Recipes from the Women of Theresienstadt." In *Food as Communication, Communication as Food*, edited by Janet M. Cramer, Carlnita P. Greene, and Lynn M. Walters. New York: Peter Lang, 137–54.

Gilbert, Sandra. 2014. *The Culinary Imagination*. New York: Norton.

Ginsberg, Stanley. 2011. *Inside the Jewish Bakery*. Philadelphia: Camino Books.

Goldin, Farideh. 2003. *Wedding Song: Memoirs of an Iranian Jewish Woman*. Hanover, England: Brandeis University Press.

Goldstein, B. David. 2018. "Commensality." In *Food and Literature*, edited by Gitanjali G. Shahani, 39–58. Cambridge: Cambridge University Press.

Goode, Judith. 1992. "Food." In *Folklore, Cultural Performances and Popular Entertainments*, edited by Richard Bauman, 233–45. New York: Oxford University Press.

Greenbaum, Abraham. [N.d.] "Traditional Education of East European Jewish Women: The Generations before the First World War." *American Association for Polish-Jewish Studies*. Accessed December 30, 2020. http://www.aapjstudies.org/index.php?id=108.

Gregory, Susan. 1999. "Gender Roles and Food in Families." In *Gender, Power and the Household*, edited by Linda McKie, Sophia Bowlby, Susan Gregory, and Jo Campling, 69–75. London: Palgrave Macmillan.

Grimes, Ronald L. 1995. *Beginnings in Ritual Studies*. Columbia: University of South Carolina Press.

Harris, Marvin. 1975. *Cows, Pigs, Wars, and Witches: The Riddles of Culture*. New York: Vintage.

———. 1987. *The Sacred Cow and the Abominable Pig: Riddles of Food and Culture*. New York: Simon and Schuster.

Hartman, David, and Diane Zimberoff. 2009. "The Hero's Journey of Self-Transformation: Models of Higher Development from Mythology." *Journal of Heart-Centered Therapies* 12, no. 2: 3–93.

Hasan-Rokem, Galit. 1978. "Proverbs in Folktales." [In Hebrew.] PhD diss., Hebrew University.

———. 1998. "The Birth of Scholarship out of the Spirit of Oral Tradition: Folk Narrative Publications and National Identity in Modern Israel." *Fabula* 39, no. 3–4: 277–90.

———. 1999. "Textualizing the Tales of the People of the Book: Folk Narrative Anthologies and National Identity." *Prooftexts* 19, no. 1: 71–82.

———. 2000. *Web of Life: Folklore and Midrash in Rabbinic Literature*. Stanford, CA: Stanford University Press.

———. 2003. *Tales of the Neighborhood*. Berkeley: University of California Press.

Hasan-Rokem, Galit, and Eli Yassif. 1989. "The Study of Jewish Folklore in Israel." *Jewish Folklore and Ethnology Review* 11, nos. 1–2: 2–11.

Held, Michal. 2009. *Let Me Tell You a Story/Vent e kontare*. [In Hebrew.] Jerusalem: Yad Ben Zvi.

Hess, M. Lisa. 2012. "Encountering Habits of Mind at Table." *CrossCurrents* 62, no. 3: 328–36.

Hevlin, Rina. 2009. *Jewish-Israeli Time*. [In Hebrew.] Tel Aviv: Hakibbutz Hameuchad.

Holland, Shmil. 2011. *Schmaltz*. [In Hebrew.] Ben Shemen, Israel: Karpad-Modan.

Holtzman, Jon D. 2006. "Food and Memory." *Annual Review of Anthropology* 35: 361–78.

Horowitz, Elliott. 2014. "Remembering the Fish and Making a Tsimmes: Jewish Food, Jewish Identity, and Jewish Memory." *Jewish Quarterly Review* 104, no. 1: 57–79.

Jacobs, Louis. 1979. "Eating as an Act of Worship in Hasidic Thought." In *Studies in Jewish Religious and Intellectual History*, edited by Siegfried Stein and Raphael Loewe, 157–66. Tuscaloosa: University of Alabama Press.

Jason, Heda, and Schoschana Gassmann. 1976. *Maerchen aus Israel*. Duesseldorf, Germany: Eugen Diederichs Verlag.

Jochnowitz, Eve. 2011. "All You Need Is a Potato: The Culinary Performances of Grushenka Abramova." *Women and Performance: A Journal of Feminist Theory* 21, no. 3, special issue: Food Legacies: 367–84.

———. 2013. "Food and Foodways." In *Encyclopedia of Jewish Folklore and Traditions*, edited by Haya Bar-Itzhak, 1:195–97. New York: M. E. Sharpe.

———. 2015. "Foodscapes: The Culinary Landscapes of Russian-Jewish New York," In *The Food and Folklore Reader*, edited by Lucy Long, 306–16. London: Bloomsbury Academic.

Jones, Ernest. 1923. *Essays in Applied Psycho-Analysis*. London: International Psycho-Analytical Press.

Jones, Michael Owen. 2000. "What's Disgusting, Why, and What Does It Matter?" *Journal of Folklore Research* 37, no. 1 (2000): 53–71.

———. 2007. "Food Choice, Symbolism, and Identity: Bread-and-Butter Issues for Folkloristics and Nutrition Studies." *Journal of American Folklore* 120, no. 476: 129–77.

Julier, Alice P. 2013. *Eating Together: Food, Friendship, and Inequality*. Champaign: University of Illinois Press.

Kauffman, Tsippi. 2009. *In All Your Ways Know Him: The Concept of God and Avodah be-Gashmiyut in the Early Stages of Hasidism*. [In Hebrew.] Ramat Gan, Israel: Bar Ilan University Press.

Kaufman, Cathy K. 2006. *Cooking in the Ancient Civilizations*. Westport, CT: Greenwood Press.

Keeling, Kara K., and Scott T. Pollard. 2020. *Table Lands: Food in Children's Literature*. Jackson: University Press of Mississippi.

Kirshenblatt-Gimblett, Barbara. 2010. "Food and Drink." In YIVO *Encyclopedia of Jews in Eastern Europe*, 529–38. http://www.yivoencyclopedia.org/printarticle.aspx?id=2098.

Klein, Alexander. 2006. "You Shall Kindle No Fire: The Interpretative Problem and Its Results." [In Hebrew.] *Weekly Page*, 645. Ramat Gan, Israel: Bar Ilan University.

Klier, John. 2011. *Russians, Jews, and the Pogroms of 1881–1882*. Cambridge: Cambridge University Press.

Korut, M. K. 1923. "Bohuslaw (Kiev Province) and Vicinity." [In Hebrew.] *Rashumot* 3: 140–57.

Kraemer, David. 2007. *Jewish Eating and Identity through the Ages*. New York: Routledge.

Kretshnif, Rabbi Eliezer Zeev. N.d. *Arbaa Arazim*. Bnei Brak, Israel: n.p.

Kurlansky, Mark. 2002. *Salt: A World History*. New York: Penguin.

Lang, Sharon. 2002. "*Sulha* Peacemaking and the Politics of Persuasion." *Journal of Palestine Studies* 31, no. 3: 52–66.

Laznow, Jacqueline. 2017. "Folklore, Tradition, and Memory among Women from the Jewish Community in Argentina." [In Hebrew.] Ph.D. diss., Hebrew University.

———. 2019. "I Recognized the Holidays According to the Food: Tradition and Memory in the Jewish Community of Argentina." [In Hebrew.] *Jerusalem Studies in Jewish Folklore* 32: 185–215.

Lévi-Strauss, Claude. 1969. *The Raw and the Cooked*. New York: Harper and Row.

———. 1997. "The Culinary Triangle." In *Food and Culture: A Reader*, edited by Carole Counihan and Penny Van Esterik, 28–35. New York: Routledge.

Levy-Mellul, Rivka. 1982. *Moroccan Cooking*. [In Hebrew.] Jerusalem: Jerusalem Publishing House.

Liebes, Yehuda. 1986. "The Shofar Voice's Angel and Joshua the Archangel." [In Hebrew.] *Jerusalem Studies in Jewish Thought* 6: 171–95. http://liebes .huji.ac.il/files/sarhapanim.pdf.

Loichot, Valerie. 2018. "The Ethics of Eating Together: The Case of French Postcolonial Literature." In *Food and Literature*, edited by Gitanjali G. Shahani, 169–85. Cambridge: Cambridge University Press.

Long, Lucy M. 2015. *The Food and Folklore Reader*. London: Bloomsbury Academic.

Luthi, Max. 1970. *Once Upon a Time: On the Nature of Fairy Tales*. New York: Frederick Ungar Publishing Company.

Marks, Gil. 2010. "Salt." In *Encyclopedia of Jewish Food*, 521–23. New York: Wiley.

Meron, Joram. 2005–12. *Village Tales: Anthology of Arab Folk Tales*. [In Hebrew.] 2 vols. Jerusalem: Minerva and Givat Haviva.

Meyer, John C. 2000. "Humor as a Double-Edged Sword: Four Functions of Humor in Communication." *Communication Theory* 10, no. 3: 310–31.

Milo, Haya. 2008. "Commentary on the tale 'The Princess in the Wooden Body' (IFA 6859)." [In Hebrew.] In *The Power of a Tale*, edited by Haya Bar-Itzhak and Idit Pintel-Ginsberg, 122–27. Haifa, Israel: University of Haifa.

———. 2019. *A Golden Kiss: Thirty-Eight Folk Tales Told by Ethiopian Jews in Israel*. [In Hebrew and Amharic.] Haifa, Israel: Pardes.

Mintz, S. W., and C. M. Du Bois. 2002. "The Anthropology of Food and Eating." *Annual Review of Anthropology* 31: 99–119.

Montanari, Massimo. 2006. *Food Is Culture*. New York: Columbia University Press.

Muhawi, Ibrahim, and Sharif Kanaana. 1989. *Speak Bird, Speak Again, Palestinian Arab Folktales*. Berkeley: University of California Press. http://publishing.cdlib.org/ucpressebooks/view?docId=ft4s2005r4&chunk.id=d0e936&toc.depth=1&toc.id=d0e936&brand=ucpress.

Myerhoff, Barbara. 1978. "Bobbes and Zeydes: Old and New Roles for Elderly Jews." In *Women in Ritual and Symbolic Roles*, edited by Judith Hoch-Smith and Anita Spring, 207–41. New York: Plenum Press.

Nachman of Breslov. 1968. *Likutay Maharan* [Gathering of Rabbi Nachman's teachings]. Jerusalem: Breslov Hasids.

———. 2002 *Sefer Hamidot* [Book of traits]. Jerusalem: Breslov Hasids.

Nadler, Allan. 2005. "Holy Kugel: The Sanctification of Ashkenazic Ethnic Foods in Hasidism." In *Food and Judaism*, edited by Leonard J. Greenspoon, Ronald A. Simkins, and Gerald Shapiro. Studies in Jewish Civilization, vol. 15, 193–214. Omaha, NE: Creighton University Press.

Navon, David. 1981. "The Seemingly Appropriate but Virtually Inappropriate: Notes about Characteristics of Jokes." Center for the Study of Reading. Technical report no. 223. Champaign: University of Illinois.

Neumann, Erich. 1956. *Amor and Psyche*. New York: Harper and Row.

Noy, Dov. 1963a. *Folktales of Israel*. Chicago: University of Chicago Press.

———. 1963b. *Jefet Schwili Erzaehlt, Hundertneunundsechzig jemenitische Volkserzaehlungen aufgezeichnet in Israel 1957–1960*. Berlin: Walter De Gruyter.

———. 1965a. *The Beautiful Maiden and the Three Princes*. [In Hebrew.] Tel Aviv: Am Oved.

———. 1965b. *Contes populaires racontes par des Juifs du Maroc*. Jerusalem: B'Tfutsot Hagola.

———. 1965c. *Cuentos populares narrados por Judios Marroquies*. Jerusalem: B'Tfutsot Hagola.

———. 1966a. *Contos Da Dispersao*. Sao Paulo: Editora Perspectiva.

———. 1966b. *Moroccan Jewish Folktales*. Jerusalem: B'Tfutsot Hagola.

———. 1968. *Contes populaires racontes par des Juifs de Tunisie*. Jerusalem: B'Tfutsot Hagola.

———. 1979. *Tale for Each Month, 1976–1977*. [In Hebrew.] Jerusalem: Center for Folklore Studies, Hebrew University.

Oring, Elliot. 1992. *Jokes and Their Relations*. Lexington: University Press of Kentucky.

———. 2003. *Engaging Humor*. Urbana: University of Illinois Press.

Ortner, Sherry B. 1973. "On Key Symbols." *American Anthropologist* 75, no. 4: 1338–46.

Patai, Raphael, and Tsafi Sebba-Elran. 2013. "Ba'al Shem Tov (BESHT)." In *Encyclopedia of Jewish Folklore and Traditions*, 1:57–60. New York: M. E. Sharpe.

Pintel-Ginsberg, Idit. 2013. "Lilith." In *Encyclopedia of Jewish Folklore and Traditions*, 1:332–35. New York: M. E. Sharpe.

Ran, Leyzer. 1987. "Vilna, Jerusalem of Lithuania." Oxford Centre for Postgraduate Hebrew Studies. http://www.ochjs.ac.uk/wp-content/uploads/2011/09/4th-Stencl-Lecture-Vilna-Jerusalem-of-Lithuania.pdf.

Rappaport, Roy A. 2002. *Ritual and Religion in the Making of Humanity*. Cambridge: Cambridge University Press.

Roden, Claudia. 1980. *A Book of Middle Eastern Food*. [In Hebrew.] Tel Aviv: Bayit Va-Gan.

———. 1999a. *The Book of Jewish Food: An Odyssey from Samarkand to New York*. New York: Penguin.

———. 1999b. "Culinary Legacies from Spain and Portugal." In *The Proceedings of the Tenth British Conference on Judeo-Spanish Studies*, edited by Annette Benaim, 257–64. London: Department of Hispanic Studies, Queen Mary and Westfield College.

Rosenblum, Jordan D. 2010a. *Food and Identity in Early Rabbinic Judaism*. New York: Cambridge University Press.

———. 2010b. " 'Why Do You Refuse to Eat Pork?': Jews, Food, and Identity in Roman Palestine." *Jewish Quarterly Review* 100, no. 1: 95–110.

Rudin, Shay. 2008. "Commentary on the Tale The Blood Libel on Passover Eve in Herat, Afganistan." [In Hebrew.] In *The Power of a Tale*, edited by Haya Bar-Itzhak and Idit Pintel-Ginsberg, 47–55. Haifa, Israel: University of Haifa Press.

Rush, Barbara. 1994. *The Book of Jewish Women's Tales*. Northvale, NJ: Jason Aronson.

Saotome, Mitsugi. 2013. *Aikado and the Harmony of Nature*. Boston: Shambhala.

Sartre, Jean Paul. 1947. *Huis Clos*. Paris: Gallimard.

Schrire, Dani. 2011. "Collecting the Pieces of Exile: A Critical View of Folklore Research in Israel in the 1940s–1950s." [In Hebrew.] PhD diss., Hebrew University.

Schwarzbaum, Haim. 1968. *Studies in Jewish and World Folklore*. Berlin: Walter de Gruyter.

Segal, Eliezer. 2014. "Judaism and Food." In *Encyclopedia of Food and Agricultural Ethics*, edited by P. B. Thompson and D. M. Kaplan, 1696–1702. Dordrecht, Netherlands: Springer.

Selwyn, Tom. 2000. "An Anthropology of Hospitality." In *In Search of Hospitality*, edited by Conrad Lashley and Alison J. Morrison, 18–37. Oxford: Butterworth-Heinemann.

Seneca, Lucius Annaeus. 1917–25. *Moral Epistles*. 3 volumes. Translated by Richard M. Gummere. Loeb Classical Library. Cambridge: Harvard University Press. http://www.stoics.com/seneca_epistles_book_1.html#'XLVII1.

Sered Starr, Susan. 1988. "Food and Holiness: Cooking as a Sacred Act among Middle-Eastern Jewish Women." *Anthropological Quarterly* 61, no. 3: 129–39.

———. 1992. *Women as Ritual Experts*. New York: Oxford University Press.

Shahani, Gitanjali G. 2018. *Food and Literature*. Cambridge: Cambridge University Press.

Shenhar, Aliza. 1974. "Family Confrontation and Conflicts in Jewish Folktales." [In Hebrew.] PhD diss., Hebrew University.

———. 1987. *Jewish and Israeli Folklore*. New Delhi: South Asian Publication.

Shkalim, Esther. 2006. "Hosting and Kitchen Culture." [In Hebrew.] In *Jewish Diaspora in the East in the 19th and the 20th century, Iran*, edited by Haim Saadon, 241–52. Jerusalem: Yad Ben Zvi.

Simon, Rachel.1992. *Change within Tradition among Jewish Women in Libya*. Seattle: University of Washington Press.

Stein, Dina. 2016. "Rabbinic Tales in the Israel Folktale Archives: Holy Men and Tricksters." [In Hebrew.] *Jerusalem Studies in Folklore* 30: 3–36. Jerusalem: Magnes.

Stoller, Robert J. 1968. *Sex and Gender*. New York: Science House.

Sutton, David E. 2001. *Remembrance of Repasts*. Oxford: Berg.

———. 2010. "Food and the Senses." *Annual Review of Anthropology* 39: 209–33.

Tartakower, Aryeh. 1964. "Jewish Professions in the Diaspora." [In Hebrew.] *Mahanayim* 91. Daat. www.daat.ac.il/DAAT/kitveyet/mahanaim/hamiktsoot-2.htm.

Thompson, Stith. 1955. *Motif-Index of Folk-Literature*. Vol. 2. Bloomington: Indiana University Press.

Trachtenberg, Joshua. 1977. *Jewish Magic and Superstition*. New York: Atheneum.

Turner, Victor. 1967. *The Forest of Symbols, Aspects of Ndembu Ritual*. Ithaca, NY: Cornell University Press.

Tyrnau, Isaac. 1884. *Sefer haMinhagim* [Book of customs]. Warsaw: n.p. TeachItToMe. http://www.teachittome.com/seforim2/seforim/sefer_minhagim.pdf.

Uther, Hans-Jorg. 2004. *The Types of International Folktales*. 3 vols. Helsinki: Suomalainen Tiedeakatemia, Academia Scientiarum Fennica.

Verman, Mark, and Shulamit H. Adler. 1993. "Path Jumping in the Jewish Magical Tradition." *Jewish Studies Quarterly* 1: 131–48.

Weiss, Ruhama. 2010. *Meal Tests: The Meal in the World of the Sages*. [In Hebrew.] Tel Aviv: Hakibbutz Hameuchad.

Westenhoefer, Joachim, and Volker Pudel. 1993. "Pleasure from Food: Importance for food Choice and Consequences of Deliberate Restriction." *Appetite* 20: 246–49.

Yaari, Abraham. 2002. *Sheluḥe Erets Yisrael.* [In Hebrew.] Jerusalem: Mosad ha-Rav Ḳuk.

Yassif, Eli. *The Hebrew Folktale.* 2009. Bloomington: Indiana University Press.

Yuval, Israel Jacob. 2008. *Two Nations in Your Womb: Perceptions of Jews and Christians in Late Antiquity and the Middle Ages.* Berkeley: University of California Press.

www.ingramcontent.com/pod-product-compliance
Lightning Source LLC
Chambersburg PA
CBHW031131270326
41929CB00011B/1580